THE DUTY OF MERCY

A Kinship Classic

Open thy mouth for the dumb
in the cause of all such as are
appointed to destruction.

Proverbs xxxi, 8

COVER: Naming the animals: from a fourth-century ivory.

THE DUTY OF MERCY
AND THE SIN OF CRUELTY TO BRUTE ANIMALS

Humphry Primatt

Edited by
RICHARD D. RYDER

Foreword by
JOHN AUSTIN BAKER

CENTAUR PRESS
FONTWELL   SUSSEX
1992

This first paperback edition published 1992
by Centaur Press Ltd, Fontwell, West Sussex
BN18 0TA

© Foreword John Austin Baker 1992
© Introduction Richard D. Ryder 1992

All rights reserved. No part of this book may be reprinted or reproduced or utilized in any form or by any electronic, mechanical, or other means, now known or hereafter invented, including photocopying and recording, or in any information storage or retrieval system, without permission in writing from the publishers.

**British Library Cataloguing in Publication Data:
A catalogue record for this book is available from the British Library**

ISBN 0-900001-38-0

Typeset by
Willow-Type, East Dean, Sussex PO18 0JB
Printed and bound by
Antony Rowe Ltd., Chippenham, Wiltshire SN14 6QA

CONTENTS

Foreword 9

Editor's Introduction 11

Author's Preface 15

Chapter 1 19

Chapter 2 45

Chapter 3 57

Chapter 4 69

Chapter 5 125

THE KINSHIP LIBRARY

"The cause of each and all of the evils that afflict the world is the same – the general lack of humanity, the lack of the knowledge that all sentient life is akin, and that he who injures a fellow being is in fact doing injury to himself."

Henry Salt: *Seventy Years Among Savages*

THE KINSHIP LIBRARY, to meet the growing demand from those concerned by the rising tide of human and animal suffering, offers work tracing the connection between our often lamentable behaviour toward each other, and our thoughtless and cruel exploitation of non-human species.

This aspect of humane education, given scant attention until recently, is becoming of major concern. The implications of Albert Schweitzer's perception that "until he extends the circle of his compassion to all living things, man will not himself find peace" are vital to any real growth in education. They explore the deepest level of the environmental conscience and have particular significance for students, teachers, and those most responsibly engaged in furthering the welfare and rights of animals.

The Kinship Library will present new books on the philosophy, politics and implications of those rights, and reissues of long unobtainable works of special merit, edited or introduced by modern scholars. The older reissues will be published as Kinship Classics.

Editorial advisors to The Kinship Library: Maureen Duffy; Audrey Eyton; George Hendrick; Charles Magel; Jan Morris; Tom Regan; Richard D. Ryder; Peter Singer; John Stockwell.

PUBLISHER'S NOTE

Other Kinship Library titles published or pending include:

All Heaven in a Rage by E.S. Turner.

Moral Inquiries on the Situation of Man and of Brutes by Lewis Gompertz, introduced by Peter Singer.

The Universal Kinship by J. Howard Moore, introduced by Charles R. Magel.

On Abstinence from Animal Food by Joseph Ritson, introduced by Keith Tester.

Also an edited reissue of Edward Maitland's *Life of Anna Kingsford*; John Oswald's *The Cry of Nature*; E.W.B. Nicholson's *The Rights of an Animal*; William Youatt's *The Obligation and Extent of Humanity to Brutes*; Thomas Young's *Essay on Humanity to Animals*; Henry Salt's *Seventy Years Among Savages*; E.D. Buckner's *The Immortality of Animals*; J. Howard Moore's *The New Ethics*; selections from the works of J. Todd Ferrier, Thomas Tryon, Lord (Thomas) Erskine, Howard Williams, Francis Newman, J.A. Gleizes, J.F. Newton, Pierre Lotti, J.L. Joynes, Lady Florence Dixie, William Lambe, Jeremy Bentham, Ernest Bell and others. New books by modern philosophers and writers will be announced.

FOREWORD

In the course of history humankind has inflicted more and greater suffering than all other animals put together, both on itself and on other creatures. An unprovable guess, no doubt, but a not unreasonable one. Moreover, religion by and large has prompted some of our worst atrocities; and so far as animals are concerned, Christianity has on the whole the blackest record among religions.

This makes the pioneer work of Humphry Primatt remarkable not only for a brilliance and force far in advance of its age, but also for the fact that he was a Christian Doctor of Divinity. It is a privilege to pay tribute to one who in this field so strikingly redeems the shame of the faith to which I belong, and to thank those who have made this foundation text of the modern animal rights and welfare movement available to a readership from which it has been withheld too long.

† John Austin Baker
Bishop of Salisbury
Salisbury 1992

INTRODUCTION

Late in 1976 I sat in the Bodleian Library in Oxford scanning ancient texts almost at random, searching for comments which might reveal past attitudes towards animals and their treatment. Out of one of these old books fell a little card upon which, in a Victorian hand, were written several references including: "The Duty of Mercy and the Sin of Cruelty to Brute Animals" by Humphry Primatt, D.D.

I sent for the book expecting, at best, another tortuous eighteenth-century tract. But when it came, I read it with amazement. Here, with unprecended clarity, was a complete book devoted to the moral treatment of animals and composed by a mind entirely comprehensible to my own. This little known doctor of divinity displayed in the 1770's remarkably similar thoughts to those Peter Singer, Tom Regan, Stephen Clark, Andrew Linzey, myself and others had recently been expressing in the 1970's. For me, it was tremendously exciting to make this bridge with the past and rediscover this almost forgotten pioneer. True, there had been earlier figures — Frances Quarles, Matthew Hale, Thomas Tryon, James Granger, John Hildrop and Richard Dean, for example, as well as some of the great men of letters — but these had usually left only fragmentary thoughts on the subject or writings which now appear rather dated. What is so remarkable about Primatt is that, in the book's early pages, his voice is instantly recognisable to us today. Although, in later chapters, he clothes his message in contemporary clerical garb and bolsters it with an impressive collection of Biblical references, this sermonising (perhaps the latter three quarters of the book are based upon actual sermons) *decorates* his thesis rather than forms a foundation for it. Indeed, he seems to apologise for going on at such length in quoting from Scripture, explaining that "it is necessary to pay some attention to the capacities of those who have not had the advantage of a liberal education." (P. 16.)

The crux of his position, as expounded in his remarkable preface and first chapter, is that:

"Pain is pain, whether it be inflicted on man or on beast; and the creature that suffers it, whether man or beast, being sensible of the misery of it while it lasts, suffers evil."

Very modernly, Primatt argues against speciesism by drawing the parallel with racism and points out that if animals lack the hope of an after-life their misery is made worse. He scoffs at humankind's arrogance and contends that, as animals have "similar nerves and organs of sensation" to humans, they deserve similar respect. He concludes with the rule:

"Do unto others as, in their condition, you would be done unto."

Who was Humphry Primatt? Jon Wynne Tyson is responsible for some new research into this question. With the help of John Baker, Bishop of Salisbury, and of the Salisbury Cathedral Librarian, Suzanne Eward, a reference to Primatt has been found in Venn's *Alumni Cantabrigienses* (1752 to 1900, Vol 5). From this source and from Anderson's *Fasti Mariscallanae Academiae* (Vol ii, p 85) we know that Primatt was admitted as a pensioner to Clare College, Cambridge, on July 11, 1752, having been born in London. He matriculated in Michaelmas, 1752, received his Bachelor of Arts degree in 1757, and Master of Arts in 1764. On 3 September, 1773, he was made doctor of Divinity at Aberdeen. He was Rector of Brampton in Norfolk in 1771 and Vicar of Higham in Suffolk and of Swardeston in Norfolk from 1766 to 1774. He resigned in 1774 and, "being a man of means, lived in some style at Kingston-on-Thames, 'for the honour of Aberdeen'", as he said. The date of his death appears to be unrecorded but must have been before 24 July, 1780 when his widow remarried. He bequeathed his books to the Marischal College in Aberdeen which is now part of Aberdeen University. Despite the efforts of that university's Archivist, Colin A. McLaren, no further biographical material has come to light. It can, however, be estimated that Primatt probably died in his forties, not long after the publication of this, his only known work.

Primatt was an inspiration, first to the Reverend Arthur Broome who helped to found in 1824 the Society which became the RSPCA, and secondly, to Henry Salt, the principal literary proponent of animal rights at the end of the last century, who included Primatt in his bibliography of 1892. The first edition of Primatt's work was published in 1776 during a resurgence of interest in the subject of mankind's treatment of the other animals. Broome himself published an abridged version in 1831. The last edition, as far as is known, was published by T. Constable in Edinburgh in 1834 — and this forms the text used for the present edition. In editing it, I have reduced Primatt's excessive use of capital letters and italics and gone some way towards modernising his punctuation.

Although Jeremy Bentham's famous 1789 footnote about animals — "The question is not can they *reason*? Nor, can they *talk*? But can they *suffer*?" — is sometimes cited as the start of the modern emphasis upon painience as the key to a wider morality, Humphry Primatt had staked out this position a few years earlier. This republication of Primatt's classic, after more than one hundred and fifty years, seems overdue.

Richard D. Ryder
1992 Haytor

PREFACE

However men may differ as to speculative points of religion, justice is a rule of universal extent and invariable obligation. We acknowledge this important truth in all matters in which man is concerned, but then we limit it to our own species only. And though we are able to trace the most evident marks of the Creator's wisdom and goodness, in the formation and appointment of the various classes of animals that are inferior to men, yet the consciousness of our own dignity and excellence is apt to suggest to us, that man alone, of all terrestrial animals, is the only proper object of mercy and compassion, because he is the most highly favoured and distinguished. Misled with this prejudice in our own favour, we overlook *some* of the brutes,[1] as if they were mere excrescences of nature, beneath our notice, and infinitely unworthy the care and cognisance of the Almighty; and we consider *others* of them, as made only for our service; and so long as we can apply them to our use, we are careless and indifferent as to their happiness or misery, and can hardly bring ourselves to suppose that there is any kind of duty incumbent upon us toward them.

---

[1] In the ensuing treatise I use the word brute as a general term for every creature inferior to man, whether beast, or bird, or fish, or fly, or worm. H.P.
'Brute' derives from the Latin 'brutus', meaning 'heavy' or 'irrational'. In eighteenth-century parlance it lacked some of its modern negative connotation and was commonly used to denote any 'irrational' animal. Johnson defines it — "An irrational creature; a creature without reason; a savage." The word 'beast' was used in a more restricted sense which did not usually include birds, fish or insects. R.D.R.

PREFACE

To rectify this mistaken notion is the design of this treatise, in which I have endeavoured to prove that as the love and mercy of God are over all his works, from the highest rational to the lowest sensitive, our love and mercy are not to be confined within the circle of our own friends, acquaintance, and neighbours; nor limited to the more enlarged sphere of human nature, to creatures of our own rank, shape, and capacity; but are to be extended to every object of the love and mercy of God, the universal parent; who, as he is righteous in all his ways, and holy in all his works, will undoubtedly require of man, superior man, a strict account of his conduct to every creature entrusted to his care, or coming in his way; and who will avenge every instance of wanton cruelty and oppression, in the day in the which he will judge the world in righteousness.

As it is of no consequence to the brutes, for whose sakes this treatise is published, what may be the different modes of faith or forms of worship amongst men, I have endeavoured to write it without any bias, prejudice, or partiality. And if some of my sentiments should not in all respects square with those of my reader, I have only to desire that they may be read and interpreted with the same candour and charity with which they are written, as I do assure him I have no design to offend any party whatsoever.

As to the manner in which this work is executed, let it be considered that, as it treats upon a subject in which men of all ranks are concerned, it is necessary to pay some attention to the capacities of those who have not had the advantage of a liberal education; and on their account it is, that the author has *enlarged* upon some points of duty in his illustration of some of the testimonies from scripture; and if it is written so as to contribute to mollify one single heart, or to rescue but a fly or a worm from unnecessary pain, it would be a reflection upon the humanity of the learned to attempt an apology for the manner of it.

But if I should seem to them to have mistaken, misapplied, or distorted any text of scripture, I hope no mistake, inaccuracy, or defect, on my part, will be any objection to the benevolent cause which I have espoused. Upon me be the reproach: spare but the innocent brute. You are welcome to say, if you please, that I have handled the word of God *improperly* or *injudiciously*, but say not that I have handled it *deceitfully*; for I am conscious my intention is good; and, if I have deceived myself, it is a delightful deception, and I should be sorry to be undeceived. But I presume I have deceived neither myself nor others, for mercy is a most amiable disposition of mind, admired even by those who will not practise it; and the cultivation of it in the lowest instances, and to the most insignificant objects, can never be attended with any ill consequences to society, nor has it any thing in it inconsistent with reason, or with our ideas of justice. Rest it upon these common principles, and, though I should have failed in my proofs from revelation, my end is in part answered, and I am well pleased; but much happier shall I be if I have been able to prove that mercy to brutes is as much a doctrine of divine revelation, as it is in itself reasonable, amiable, useful, and just.

CHAPTER ONE

LOVE is the great hinge upon which universal nature turns. The Creation is a transcript of the divine goodness; and every leaf in the "Book of Nature" reads us a lecture on the wisdom and benevolence of its great author. The philosopher[1], inured to study and contemplation, untainted with pride, and unbiased by prejudice, sees and acknowledges this truth as incontestable, that the Supreme Being is wise, and just, and good, and merciful. And from the observations he has made upon the animal part of the creation that is within his view and reach, he draws this general conclusion, that every creature must have its proper use and office, however latent as to us; and that the different powers, appetites, perfections, and even comparative defects of different animals, are essentially necessary to answer the different purposes for which they were created, and to promote the common good of the whole. I shall not undertake to illustrate this particular, as it would carry me too far from my purpose, and as all that I could say would be but a repetition of what has already been written by the many learned and ingenious naturalists, whose sole aim it has been to demonstrate the existence and perfections of God from the works of Creation. I shall therefore take it for granted, that as God is wise and good, all his works and appointments must be the effects of wisdom and goodness.

Upon this principle, every creature of God is good in its kind; that is, it is such as it ought to be. For to suppose otherwise, is to arraign the divine wisdom for making it such as it is. And as every creature is good in

---

[1] Here Primatt appears to be referring to Aristotle. R.D.R.

its kind, and did not make itself what it is, but is such as it is solely by the will and appointment of God, it follows that, whatever its perfections or defects may be, they cannot be owing to any merit or demerit in the creature itself, being, not prior, but consequential to its creation. There is not therefore in nature any foundation for pride on account of perfection, nor for contempt on account of defect. Subordination is as necessary in the natural, as in the political world; it connects the whole together, and makes the creatures dependent upon, and subservient to each other; and it preserves that harmony, variety, beauty, and good order, which would be lost in a perfect sameness and equality.

Every creature is to be considered as a wheel in the great machinery of nature; and if the whole machine is curious and beautiful, no wheel in it, however small, can be contemptible or useless. In some animals, their usefulness, which to us is their perfection, is subservient and owing to their defects. Consequently, to despise or abuse them for being defective, is to despise or abuse them for being useful. The most ugly animals, though we knew no other use of them, may be considered as a foil, like the shades in a good picture, to set off the beauties of the more perfect. And even the loathsome vermin are not without their use, when they compel us to preserve neatness and cleanliness in our houses and persons.

An animal, whatever it be, or wherever it is placed in the great scale of being, is such, and is so placed by the great Creator and Father of the universe. At the top of the scale of terrestrial animals we suppose man; and when we contemplate the perfections of body, and the endowments of mind which, we presume, he possesses above all the other animals, we justly suppose him there constituted by his Maker. But, in this *highest* rank, we may observe degrees and differences, not only as to stature, beauty, strength, and complexion, but also as to those very powers of the mind, which so eminently distinguish men from brutes. Yet, in *one* particular we all agree alike, from the most perfect to the most dull and deformed of men, and from him down to the vilest brute, that we are all susceptible and sensible of the misery of *pain*; an evil, which, though necessary in itself, and wisely intended as the spur to incite us to self-preservation, and to the avoidance of destruction, we nevertheless are naturally adverse to, and shrink back at the apprehension of it. Superiority of rank or station exempts no creature from the sensibility of pain, not does inferiority render the feelings thereof the less exquisite. Pain is pain, whether it be inflicted on man or on beast; and the creature that suffers it, whether man or beast, being sensible of the misery of it whilst it lasts, suffers *evil*; and the sufferance of evil, unmeritedly, unprovokedly, where no offence has been given, and no good end can possibly be answered by it, but merely to exhibit power or gratify malice, is cruelty and injustice in him that occasions it.

I presume there is no man of feeling, that has any idea of justice, but would confess upon the principles of reason and common sense, that if he were to be put to unnecessary and unmerited pain by another man, his tormentor would do him an act of injustice; and from a sense of the injustice in his own case, now that he is the sufferer, he must naturally infer, that if he were to put another man of feeling to the same unnecessary and unmerited pain which he now suffers, the injustice in himself to the other would be exactly the same as the injustice in his tormentor to him. Therefore the man of feeling and justice will not put another man to unmerited pain, because he will not do that to another, which he is unwilling should be done to himself. Nor will he take any advantage of his own superiority of strength, or of the accidents of fortune, to abuse them to the oppression of his inferior; because he knows that in the article of *feeling* all men are equal; and that the differences of strength or station are as much the gifts and appointments of God, as the differences of understanding, colour, or stature. Superiority of rank or station may give ability to communicate happiness, and seems so intended; but it can give no right to inflict unnecessary or unmerited pain. A wise man would impeach his own wisdom, and be unworthy of the blessing of a good understanding, if he were to infer from thence that he had a right to despise or make game of a fool, or put him to any degree of pain. The folly of the fool ought rather to excite his compassion, and demands the wise man's care and attention to one that cannot take care of himself.

It has pleased God the father of all men, to cover some men with white skins, and others with black skins; but as there is neither merit nor demerit in complexion, the white man, notwithstanding the barbarity of custom and prejudice, can have no right, by virtue of his colour, to enslave and tyrannise over a black man; nor has a fair man any right to despise, abuse, and insult a brown man. Nor do I believe that a tall man, by virtue of his stature, has any legal right to trample a dwarf under his foot. For, whether a man is wise or foolish, white or black, fair or brown, tall or short, and I might add, rich or poor, for it is no more a man's choice to be poor, than it is to be a fool, or a dwarf, or black, or tawny, such he is by God's appointment; and, abstractedly considered, is neither a subject for pride, nor an object of contempt. Now, if amongst men, the differences of their powers of the mind, and of their complexion, stature, and accidents of fortune, do not give any one man a right to abuse or insult any other man on account of these differences, for the same reason, a man can have no natural right to abuse and torment a beast, merely because a beast has not the mental powers of a man. For, such as the man is, he is but as God made him; and the very same is true of the beast. Neither of them can lay claim to any intrinsic merit, for being such as they are; for, before they were created, it was impossible that either of them could deserve; and at their creation, their shapes, perfections, or defects were invariably fixed, and their bounds set which they cannot pass. And being such, neither more nor less than God made them, there is no more demerit in a beast being a beast, than there is merit in a man being a man; that it, there is neither merit nor demerit in either of them.

A brute is an animal no less sensible of pain than a man. He has similar nerves and organs of sensation; and his cries and groans, in case of violent impressions upon his body, though he cannot utter his complaints by speech, or human voice, are as strong indications to us of his sensibility of pain, as the cries and groans of a human being, whose language we do not understand. Now, as pain is what we are all averse to, our own sensibility of pain should teach us to commiserate it in others, to alleviate it if possible, but never wantonly or unmeritedly to inflict it. As the differences amongst men in the above particulars are no bars to their feelings, so neither does the difference of the shape of a brute from that of a man exempt the brute from feeling; at least, we have no ground to suppose it. But shape or figure is as much the appointment of God, as complexion or stature. And if the difference of complexion or stature does not convey to one man a right to despise and abuse another man, the difference of shape between a man and a brute, cannot give to a man any right to abuse and torment a brute. For he that made man and man to differ in complexion or stature, made man and brute to differ in shape or figure. And in this case likewise there is neither merit nor demerit; every creature, whether man or brute, bearing that shape which the supreme Wisdom judged most expedient to answer the end for which the creature was ordained.

With regard to the modification of the mass of matter of which an animal is formed, it is accidental as to the creature itself. I mean, it was not in the power or will of the creature to choose whether it should sustain the shape of a brute or of a man: and yet, whether it be of one shape or of the other; or whether it be inhabited or animated by the soul[1] of a brute or the soul of a man; the substance or matter of which the creature is composed would be equally susceptible of feeling. It is

---

[1] It is of no consequence as to the case now before us, whether the soul is, as some think, only a power, which cannot exist without the body; or as is generally supposed, a spiritual substance, that can exist, distinct and separate from the body. H.P.

THE DUTY OF MERCY

solely owing to the good pleasure of God, that we are created men, or animals in the *shape* of men. For he that formed[1] man of the dust of the ground, and breathed into his nostrils the breath of life, that he might become a living soul, and endued with the sense of feeling, could, if he had so pleased, by the same plastic power, have cast the very same dust into the mould of a beast; which, being animated by the life-giving breath of its Maker, would have become a living soul[2] in that form; and, in that form, would have been as susceptible of pain, as in the form of a man. And if, in brutal shape, we had been endued with the same degree of reason and reflection which we now enjoy; and other beings, in human shape, should take upon them to torment, abuse, and barbarously ill-treat us, because we were not made in their shape; the injustice and cruelty of their behaviour to us would be self-evident, and we should naturally infer that – whether we walk upon two legs or four, whether our heads are prone or erect, whether we are naked or covered with hair, whether we have tails or no tails, horns or no horns, long ears or round ears; or whether we bray like an ass, speak like a man, whistle like a bird, or are mute as a fish – nature never intended these distinctions as foundations for right of tyranny and oppression. But, perhaps, it will be said it is absurd to make such an inference from a mere supposition that a man *might* have been a brute, and a brute *might* have been a man; for the supposition itself is chimerical, and has no foundation in nature; and all arguments should be drawn from fact, and not from fancy of what might be or might not be. To this I reply in few words, and in general: that all cases and arguments, deduced from the important and benevolent precept of *doing to others as we would be done unto*, necessarily require such kind of suppositions; that is, they suppose the case to be otherwise than it really is. For instance, a rich man

---

[1] Gen. ii. 7.
[2] Gen. i. 30. In the margin.

is not a poor man; yet, the duty plainly arising from the precept is this: the man who is now *rich* ought to behave to the man who is now *poor*, in such a manner as the rich man, *if he were poor*, would be willing that the poor man, *if he were rich*, should behave towards him. Here is a case which in fact does not exist between these two men, for the rich man is not a poor man, nor is the poor man a rich man; yet the *supposition* is necessary to enforce and illustrate the precept, and the reasonableness of it is allowed. And if the supposition is reasonable in one case, it is reasonable – at least, not contrary to reason – in all cases to which this general precept can extend, and in which the duty enjoined by it can and ought to be performed. Therefore, though it be true that a man is not a horse, yet, as a horse is a subject within the extent of the precept, that is, he is capable of receiving benefit by it, the duty enjoined in it extends to the man, and amounts to this: do you that are a man so treat your horse, as you would be willing to be treated by your master, in case that you *were* a horse. I see no absurdity nor false reasoning in this precept, nor any ill consequence that would arise from it, however it may be gainsaid by the barbarity of custom.

But there is no custom, whether barbarous or absurd, nor indeed any vice, however detestable, but will find some abettors to justify, or at least, to palliate it; though the vindication itself is an aggravation of the crime. When we are under apprehensions that we ourselves shall be the sufferers of pain, we naturally shrink back at the very idea of it; we can then abominate it, we detest it with horror, we plead hard for mercy, and we feel that *we can feel*. But when man is out of the question, humanity sleeps, and the heart grows callous. We no longer consider ourselves as creatures of sense, but as lords of the creation. Pride, prejudice, aversion to singularity, and contracted misrepresentations of God and religion, do all contribute to harden the heart against the natural impressions and soft feelings of compassion. And when the mind is thus warped and disposed to evil, a light argument will have great weight with it, and we ransack and rack all nature in her weakest and tenderest parts, to extort from her, if possible, any confession whereon to rest the appearance of an argument to defend or excuse our cruelty and oppression.

The consciousness of the rank which, as men, we hold in the creation, and of the evidently superior powers of the mind of man, which justly distinguish men from brutes, puff us up with such a fond conceit of our own dignity and merit, that to make any comparison between a man and a brute is deemed as absurd as it is odious, and hurtful to our pride.

The mistaken indulgence of parents, and the various instances of sportive cruelty, in some shape or other daily practised by men in all ranks of life; and the many barbarous customs connived at, if not countenanced by persons in high stations or in great authority (whose conduct in other points may be truly amiable and respectable), prejudice our minds to consider the brute animals as senseless and insignificant creatures, made only for our pleasure and sport. And, when we reflect upon the most shocking barbarities, and see the brutal rage exercised by the most worthless of men, without control of law, and *without notice or reproof from the pulpit*[1], we are almost tempted to draw this inference, that *cruelty cannot be sin*.

And, possibly, the affectation of love or hatred according to the mode of the fashion (in other words, *vicious taste*, which consists in making the love or hatred of others the standard of our own love and hatred; that we must admire whatever our superiors admire, and condemn whatever they are pleased to condemn; that true politeness is to have no thought, no soul, no

---

[1] The Reverend James Granger had preached a sermon against cruelty to animals to his Shiplake parishioners on 18 October 1772. It was received with 'almost universal disgust,' but was published in London later the same year. (See Richard D. Ryder, *Animal Revolution; Changing Attitudes to Speciesism*, Blackwell, 1989). R.D.R.

sentiment of our own, but a graceful resignation of the plainest dictates of truth and common sense to the follies and whims of others; that the art of pleasing is the art of flattery and base compliance; and the singularity of sentiment or practice is the mark of a mean, a vulgar, and a churlish soul) – this affectation of compliance, this vicious taste, and this aversion to singularity, may possibly lead us to suppose that no diversion can be cruel that has the sanction of nobility and that no dish can be unblessed that is served up at a great man's table, though *the kitchen is covered with blood, and filled with the cries of creatures expiring in tortures.*[1]

I am sorry there should be any occasion to name religion as in any respect contributing to this insensibility and indifference as to the happiness or misery of the inferior animals. I am well aware of her delicacy and tenderness; and hope I shall not be deemed rude or uncharitable, or as reflecting upon true religion, when I declare it is not my intention to give offence to Christians of any denomination. Let me not then be misunderstood, when I express the concern of my soul if her sacred garments have ever been polluted with blood, unless misrepresented. But upon inquiry, we fear it is too true that there have been professors of religion who thought they did God service when they defaced his image; and anathematized with the most bitter imprecations, and persecuted with torture even unto death, unhappy wretches whose misfortune it was to suppose their souls were their own, or whose only crime it was to *have more understanding than all their teachers.*[2] Now, is it possible that compassion to brutes

---

[1] The Guardian, Vol. i. No. 61.
Primatt is here referring to an article contributed to the Guardian of May 21, 1713, by Alexander Pope, which is devoted entirely to attacking cruelty to animals. Joseph Addison and Richard Steele had preceded him with similar pieces, and these distinguished men heralded the eighteenth-century awakening of interest in the subject. R.D.R.
[2] Psalm cxix. 99.

could find place in a breast that withheld and denied the mercy of God unto men? Or, are we to wonder that cruelty to brutes made no article of self-examination, when mercy itself was deemed heresy? Even in prior and purer times, it was affirmed that it is absurd,[1] and a disparagement to the majesty of God, to suppose Him to know how many insects there are in the world, or how many fishes in the sea; yea, that such an idea of the omniscience of God would be foolish flattery to Him, and an injury to ourselves. Now, if God knows them not, he cannot regard them; and if He regards them not, why should we? Why should we thus flatter God, and injure our own pride?

But let not these mistaken notions be imputed to the spirit of the Gospel of Jesus. Love and benevolence are the genuine characteristics of his religion, which originated in the mercy of God, and is perfected in the love of man. True Christian humility abominates these swellings of spiritual pride, and the enlarged soul of a Christian cannot find room in the narrow heart of a bigot. I mean not to give offence to any one; but if any take offence, they bespeak the error I mean to correct. Christian love is without partiality, and without hypocrisy, and all that I mean is this: let not our love be evil spoken of; let us examine ourselves well, and if we find that we hold any doctrine or tenet that explicitly or consequentially represents the supreme being as partial or injurious to any of his creatures, such doctrine is a contracted misrepresentation of the divine goodness, and must have a natural tendency to erase from the human mind all ideas of justice and mercy to creatures of inferior orders.

I said above, that pride, prejudice, aversion to singu-

---

[1] Absurdum est ad hoc Die deducere Majestatem, ut sciat per momenta singula quot nascantur culices, quotve moriantur; quæ cimicum et pulicum et muscarum sit in terra multitudo; quanti pisces in aqua natent, et qui de minoribus majorum prædæ cedere debeant. Non simus tam fatui Adulatores Dei, ut dum potentiam ejus etiam ad ima detrahimus in nos ipsos injuriosi simus. Hieronymi, *Comment. in Abac. Lib. 1. Edit. Basil. Tom. vi. p. 187.*

larity, and contracted misrepresentations of God and religion, do all contribute to harden the heart against the natural impressions and soft feelings of compassion. But perhaps I may be mistaken as to the three last particulars; at least, there are very few persons who will ingenuously confess themselves the dupes of prejudice, or the fools of affectation; and as to mistakes in points of religion, they are scarce ever acknowledged, hard to be rectified, and hardly to be touched upon, though with the utmost tenderness, without exciting the flame, which it is the scope of true religion to quench and suppress. But as to pride, which arises from the fond conceit of our own dignity and superior excellence above the brutes; though the name is odious, and we disclaim the imputation of it, yet we cherish it with pleasure, and dote upon it with admiration. We blush at the thought of a comparison; we fire with resentment; we toss up our heads with scorn, and claim kindred with heaven.

Well; be it so. Man is the most noble, the most excellent, the most perfect of all terrestrial beings. But what then? He is still but a creature; and, with all his perfections and excellencies, he is a dependent and accountable creature; yea, accountable for these very perfections and excellencies, whether or no he has behaved in a manner becoming a creature so eminently distinguished and exalted. And, if found deficient in this grand inquisition, that wherein he now glories will be the burthen of his disgrace. The more talents are intrusted with any man, the more he stands accountable for; and if not rightly employed, or misapplied, it had been better for him not to have possessed them.

Every excellence in a man is surcharged with a duty, from which the superiority of his station cannot exempt him. Nay, his superior station urges the demand and his non-compliance may be justly deemed stubbornness and ingratitude. And where superiority of station, and excellence of nature, do both concur in one subject (as is sometimes, but not always, the case amongst men), there the duty required is greater, and the obligation is stronger. But, however it may be between man and man, this is certain, that when we compare man and brute, we find both excellence and superiority to centre in man. The excellence of the nature of a man to that of a brute, no one will question; and the advantages which the lowest of men derive from their station as men, give them a superiority which deserves their gratitude and attention. This granted, I believe it will be found not dissonant from reason, if we were to affirm from the above principle, that the cruelty of men to brutes is more heinous (in point of justice) than the cruelty of men unto men. I will call the former *brutal* cruelty, and the latter *human* cruelty.

In the case of *human* cruelty, the oppressed man has a tongue that can plead his own cause, and a finger to point out the aggressor: all men that hear of it shudder with horror and, by applying the case to themselves, pronounce it *cruelty* with the common voice of humanity, and unanimously join in demanding the punishment of the offender, and brand him with infamy. But in the case of *brutal* cruelty, the dumb beast can neither utter his complaints to his own kind, nor describe the author of his wrong; nor, if he could, have they it in their power to redress and avenge him.

In the case of human cruelty, there are courts and laws of justice in every civilized society, to which the injured man may make his appeal; the affair is canvassed, and punishment inflicted in proportion to the offence. But alas! with shame to man, and sorrow for brute, I ask the question: what laws are now in force, or what court of judicature does now exist, in which the suffering brute may bring his action against the wanton cruelty of barbarous man? The laws of Triptolemus[1] are long since buried in oblivion, for Triptolemus was but a heathen. No friend, no advocate, not one, is to be found amongst the bulls nor calves[2] of the people to prefer an indictment on behalf of the brute. The priest

---

[1] According to Greek legend, Triptolemus was the founder of the Eleusinian Mysteries and the inventor of the plough, and was sent about the world by Demeter to teach the art of agriculture. R.D.R.
[2] Psalm lxviii. 30.

passeth by on one side, and the Levite on the other side; the Samaritan stands still, sheds a tear, but can no more; for there is none to help; and the poor wretched and unbefriended creature is left to moan in unregarded sorrow, and to sink under the weight of his burden.

But suppose the law promulged,[1] and the court erected. The judge is seated, the jury sworn, the indictment read, the cause debated, and a verdict found for the plaintiff. Yet what cost or damage? What recompense for loss sustained? In actions of humanity, with or without law, satisfaction may be made. In various ways you can make amends to a man for the injuries you have done him. You know his wants, and you may relieve him. You may give him clothes, or food, or money. You may raise him to a higher station, and make him happier than before you afflicted him. You may be feet to the lame, and eyes to the blind. You may entertain him, keep him company, or supply him with every comfort, convenience, and amusement of life, which he is capable of enjoying. And thus may you make some atonement for the injury you have done unto a man; and by thy assiduity and future tenderness, thou mayest perhaps obtain his pardon, and palliate thine own offence. But what is all this to the injured brute? If by thy passion or malice, or sportive cruelty, thou hast broken his limbs, or deprived him of his eye-sight, how wilt thou make *him* amends? Thou canst do nothing to amuse him. He wants not thy money nor thy clothes. Thy conversation can do him no good. Thou hast obstructed his means of getting subsistence; and thou wilt hardly take upon thyself the pains and trouble of procuring it for him (which yet by the rule of justice thou art bound to do). Thou hast marred his little temporary happiness, which was his all to him. Thou hast maimed or blinded him for ever; and hast done him an *irreparable* injury.

But here it will be suggested, that there are some men in the world as unfortunately circumstanced, and as far from the means of redress, as the unhappy brute now before us. It may be so. Yet, be it remembered, that a day

---

[1] Promulgate (archaic.) R.D.R.

will come, when all the injuries which an innocent man can suffer from the hand of violence and oppression will be overbalanced in a future and happy state, where our light affliction, which, in comparison of eternity, is but for a moment, shall work for us a far more exceeding and external weight of glory. This is the hope and confidence of a *man*. And a most comfortable reflection it is indeed to the virtuous and innocent sufferer who knows that he has an almighty Patron and Avenger, who will finally cause that the malice and wickedness of his enemies here shall at length promote the degree of his glory hereafter. But what hope, what glimpse of recompense hereafter, awaiteth the afflicted *brute*? An hereafter for a brute, a recompense for a beast, has a strange sound in the ears of a man. We cannot bear the thought of it. Injustice itself is a virtue in the judgment of partiality; and in the pride of our heart we rather say: let man be happy, though all creation groan. Yet it is a truth that ought not to be concealed, that God is a righteous judge; and it is presumption in Man to determine the limits of the divine goodness. However, as we have no authority to declare, and no testimony from heaven to assure us, that there is a state of recompense for suffering brutality, we will suppose there is none; and from this very supposition we rationally infer that cruelty to a brute is an injury irreparable.

Compare the whole of both the cases together, and the difference is striking. The injured *man* has a tongue that can utter his complaints; he can appeal to the laws of his country; he may obtain redress from his own species; or if overlooked here, and debarred or denied the just and common claims of humanity, he can make his further appeal to the righteous Judge of all the earth, and, under the severest oppressions, can lift up his head with hope and confidence, in expectation of another state, wherein he shall be comforted for all the days in which he hath suffered adversity. But, on the other hand, the injured *brute* hath neither speech to plead for him, nor law to protect him, nor hope of future recompense to support him. His present life (for any thing we know) is the whole of his existence; and if he is unhappy here, his lot is truly pitiable; and the more pitiable his lot, the more base, barbarous, and unjust in man, must be every instance of cruelty towards him. To suffer pain and misery from the hand of man merely because he is a brute, he *ought* not. To suffer pain as punishment he *cannot*, for punishment is due only to demerit; and demerit, being of a moral nature, can be attributed only to *rational* beings, when they act in a manner unbecoming that station in which the providence of God hath placed them. Demerit, therefore (according to our own favourite principle, that man only is rational), is peculiar to men; and is never more conspicuous than when we despise or abuse the inferior and *irrational* part of the creation; for in no instance do we more betray our weakness, debase our pride, and act beneath the dignity of our exalted station.

When a man boasts of the dignity of his nature, and the disadvantages of his station, and then and from thence infers his right of oppression of his inferiors, he exhibits his folly as well as his malice.

What should we think of a stout and strong man, that should exert his fury and barbarity on a helpless and innocent babe? Should we not abhor and detest that man, as a mean, cowardly, and savage wretch, unworthy the stature and strength of a man? No less mean, cowardly, and savage is it to abuse and torment the innocent beast, who can neither help himself nor avenge himself, and yet has as much right to happiness in this world as a child can have; nay, more right, if this world be his only inheritance.

Again, what dignity or distinction have we, that we did not receive from the great Giver of all good? It is true that man is superior to a brute. But then, "Who maketh thee, O man, thus to differ? And what hast thou that thou didst not receive? Now, if thou didst receive it, why dost thou glory, as if thou hadst not received?"[1] "Have we not

---
[1] 1 Cor. iv. 7.

THE DUTY OF MERCY

all one Father, and hath not one God created us?"[1] He that made thee a man, could have made thee a brute. Now, if thou art a man, be thankful, and shew thy superiority by mercy and compassion; else thou debasest thy reason, and art as low, if not lower than the brute whom you oppress. You confess that a brute is *an animal without reason*; and reason says, that to put any creature to unmerited or unnecessary pain is unjust and *unreasonable*: therefore, a man that is cruel is *a brute in the shape of a man*.

But what! say you, shall a man endued with an immortal soul be compared unto a beast that perisheth? I answer, be this as it may happen. If a man acts like a brute, the comparison is just, however disagreeable. But, waving the comparison, if thou art cruel, thy boast of immortality is the most egregious folly. Thou art like a prisoner making his boast of the brightness and exquisite workmanship of his fetters. Or, thou art like an unjust and haughty steward of a great estate, counting over his lord's money, and bragging of it as if it were his own; and flattering himself with the future favour of his master, though all the tenants groan under the weight of his oppression, and can and are ready to bear witness to his pride and perfidy, at their lord's return, when a thousand articles will be exhibited against the upstart sycophant, of waste, mismanagement, negligence, abuse, tyranny, and injustice. Yet this is thine own case, this thine own folly, if thy soul is polluted with malice and cruelty. Thou mayst glory in thy pretensions to immortality now; but wilt thou glory in it hereafter, when the dreadful time shall come that thou wilt wish thyself upon a level with the beast whom thou hast despised and abused; when thine immortality will be thy greatest burthen? Strange, therefore, to hear cruel men boast of that very circumstance which will make them truly wretched.

But I know not how it is; our hands are so imbrued in blood, that, in spite of the shame of it, we cannot wash

---

[1] Mal. ii. 10.

them clean. We glory in that which, being misapplied, is our disgrace; and when we feel ourselves wounded in our pride, we change the scales; we drop the consideration of our own dignity, which avails us but little, and betake us to arguments of another kind, which are equally inconclusive when alleged in defence or excuse of the wanton cruelty of man.

For thus it is argued:

that man has a permission, that is, it is a universal practice with mankind, to eat the flesh of animals, which cannot be done without taking away their lives, and putting them to some degree of pain;

that there are some animals obnoxious to mankind, and the most compassionate of men make no scruple to destroy them;

that there are some brutes of prey which wholly subsist on the flesh of other brutes and whose lives are one continued course of rapine and bloodshed.

These are the formidable arguments which we sometimes have recourse to in vindication of our cruelty, our abuse, or unfeeling neglect; but to each I shall make a reply.

And, first, as it is a universal practice, it shall be taken for granted that man has a permission to eat the flesh of some animals, and consequently, to kill them for food or necessary use.

But this permission cannot authorise us to put them to unnecessary pain, or lingering death. Death they are all liable to; they must submit to it; and they do not seem to us to have any idea or fear of death. Avoidance of pain is indeed as natural to brutes as it is to men, therefore pain is the only ground of fear in brutes.

As to ourselves, we fear both pain and death; and our fear of death arises from the fear of future pain, or from apprehensions of what may happen to us after death; and in some men these apprehensions are so terrifying that they prefer exquisite pain to death. But the brute, having no idea of an hereafter, cannot suffer any terror on account of death. To him, present pain is the only evil, and present happiness the only good; therefore, whilst he lives he has a right to happiness. And death, though it is to him the period of his present happiness of existence (and so far is a negative evil), yet it is likewise the period to all his fears and future pain; and so far as it removes him from the possibility of future misery from the cruelty of men, it may be considered as a positive good. But be this as it may, death to a brute is nothing terrible. He must die once as well as we; and though it is of small moment whether my beast is to die today or tomorrow, yet if I will not kill him till tomorrow, I ought not to put him to pain today, for, whilst he lives, he has a right to happiness. At least I have no right to make him miserable; and, when I kill him, I ought to dispatch him suddenly, and with the least degree of pain. This is my opinion; and even if I should be mistaken, it appears to me to be false reasoning to say, that because I have permission to kill a brute, and cannot kill him without putting him to some degree of necessary pain in the short article of death, therefore I have permission to put him or any other brute to unnecessary pain in the long article of life. It is as fallacious as to say, that because the future happiness of a family may depend upon the present gentle correction of the child of it, now that he is in fault, therefore severity and moroseness are commendable and justifiable in a parent. Or, in general, that, because some pain is a necessary and unavoidable evil to promote some good, therefore all pain is good and desirable. Which would be granting too much.

But, secondly, it is alleged that there are some animals obnoxious to mankind; and the most compassionate of men make no scruple to destroy them.

It is true; some animals are obnoxious to us, and have it in their power to hurt us. But very seldom do they exert that power; and well it is for us that they have not the malice nor revenge that is in man. "It is observable (says the ingenuous writer of the *Guardian*, Vol. i. No. 61.)[1] of those noxious animals, which have qualities most powerful to injure us, that they naturally avoid

[1] Alexander Pope. See footnote on p.27. R.D.R.

mankind, and never hurt us unless provoked, or necessitated by hunger. But man, on the other hand, seeks out and pursues even the most inoffensive animals on purpose to persecute and destroy them." If this be the case, it appears that mercy preponderates in the scale of brutes. For one injury which we may possibly receive from the creatures, we offer them a thousand. A horse may now and then, when provoked, give a man an unlucky kick; but what is this to the blows, and cuts, and spurs, which they receive every day and every hour from the brutal rage and unrelenting barbarity of men? The matter of wonder is, that we do not oftener feel the effects of their power and resentment. If we consider the excruciating injuries offered on *our* part to the brutes, and the patience on *their* part; how frequent *our* provocations, and how seldom *their* resentment (and in some cases *our* weakness and *their* strength, *our* slowness and *their* swiftness), one would be almost tempted to suppose (reason to both alike allowed) that the brutes had combined in one general scheme of benevolence to teach mankind lessons of mercy, and meekness, by their own forbearance and long suffering. But grant that there are some fierce and formidable animals that are strangers to pity and compassion. Does this justify the suppression of these amiable dispositions in men? Because a wolf will seize upon a man, is a man therefore warranted to whip a pig to death? Or, because a serpent will bite a man by the heel, is a man to tread upon every harmless earthworm he sees wriggling upon the ground? No. If some offensive creatures do sometimes unprovokedly molest us, let it be accounted but as a retaliation of the injuries we offer to those that are inoffensive (and thus even the dreadful hornet may be considered but as the avenger of the sufferings of the feeble fly); for cruelty and cowardice are near of kin;[1] and we exert our power mostly upon those creatures who can neither do us an

---

[1] Cowards are cruel; but the brave
Love Mercy and delight to save.   GAY

injury, nor return an injury done. But suppose we happen to meet with noxious animals, let us prudently get out of their path. But what if I cannot avoid them? Why, then, it is time enough to put myself in a posture of defence; and, for my own preservation, I think it no more crime to defend myself from the beast or serpent, than from a villainous man that should attack my person; and if, in the fray, I kill the beast, I cannot charge myself with malice, or any intentional cruelty, provided I dispatch him as instantaneously as possible. If a wasp or a hornet comes into my room, I dread his weapon; but I hate him not: he is a beautiful insect and, I make no doubt, was created for some useful purpose. I am sorry I am necessitated to kill him; but I will not clip him in pieces with my scissors, if I can crush him under my foot. But if I cannot master him, unless I clip him, having so done, I dare not leave him in the pain of a lingering death for many hours together, but I finish the mortal work with all expedition. And in this, I hope, there is no cruelty; for cruelty in this case consists in the unnecessary infliction and continuation of pain, and not in putting the creature to instant death, which is the period of all pain. Self-preservation, therefore (whether, as in the former case, for the support of nature in the article of food; or, in the present case, for the avoidance of pain and destruction from the attacks of obnoxious animals), though it may justify a man in putting a brute to instant death, yet cannot warrant the least act of cruelty to any creature, however ferocious or savage it may be; much less can it justify the hunting out, for sport and destruction, creatures of the tamer kind, whose inability to defend themselves, whose harmless nature, and whose panting fears, rather demand all our compassion, and even our protection and attention.

Thirdly, it is alleged, that there are some brutes of prey which wholly subsist on the flesh of other brutes, and whose lives are one continued course of rapine and bloodshed.

This likewise is true; and in the present state of nature, subject to misery and decay, it seems to be the wise and good appointment of the great Creator. Were there no beasts or birds of prey, we should every day be tormented with the sight of numbers of poor creatures dying by inches (as we say) and pining away through age or accidental infirmity. And, when dead upon the ground (as men would hardly give themselves the trouble to bury them, or it would take up too much of our time to bury them all) the unburied carcasses would by their stench create such a pestilence in the air, as would not only endanger our lives and health, but would likewise be extremely offensive to us. To guard against these evils, it hath pleased God to appoint that (in some countries) lions, tigers, and eagles; and, in other countries, wolves, foxes, kites, ravens, and hawks should range the woods and fields in search of the unburied bodies, and thus become the living graves of the dead. And if, in the course of their range of flight, they espy a beast or bird worn out with age, or with a leg or wing by accident broken, or forsaken by his dam, unable to help himself, or any way rendered incapable of getting his own food; God, the Father of Mercies, hath ordained beasts and birds of prey to do that distressed creature the kindness to relieve him from his misery, by putting him to death. A kindness which we dare not shew to our own species. If thy father, thy brother, or thy child should suffer utmost pains of a long and agonizing sickness, though his groans should pierce through thy heart, and with strong crying and tears he should beg thy relief, yet thou must be deaf unto him; he must wait his appointed time till his change cometh, till he sinks and is crushed with the weight of his misery. But then, in all *human* affliction, whether our own or others (not the punishment or effect of vice and debauchery), we may comfort ourselves and them with the *hope* of a blessed immortality, when *all tears shall be wiped from our eyes; when there shall be no more death, neither sorrow nor crying, neither shall there be any more pain.*[1] Human hope is

[1] Rev. xxi. 4.

human support and comfort. But what hope is there to support and comfort the brutes under their affliction? They are incapable of hope, because they can neither reflect nor foresee. The present moment is as eternity to them. All their happiness is in this life only; they have neither thought nor hope of another. Therefore, when they are miserable, their misery is the more insupportable. And when they can no longer enjoy happiness, death is welcome; and the more welcome, the sooner it comes; and sudden death more desirable than a lingering painful life. And whilst the poor animal is thus kindly delivered from his pain by precipitated death, the creature that devours him has his degree of happiness therein, and will himself one day meet with the same kind treatment from some other beast or bird, when he is no longer able to enjoy life. This is not cruelty but mercy: as much mercy as it is to shoot thy horse or thy dog, when all his teeth are gone, and the happiness of his life is at the end.[1]

And what if some of the creatures, swifter of foot or wing than the tamer kind, should sometimes seize upon a harmless and defenceless animal not under the distressed case before supposed? This should be considered as an accidental evil hardly to be avoided in the present state of things. In brutes it is natural, and not a moral evil. Ferocity, strength, and a carnivorous appetite are essentially necessary to brutes of prey; and the divine Being does not interpose to alter their natures, if by chance they meet with a sheep or a man. It is necessary that they should be savage, to answer the purposes of their creation; else they would not have been so created. It is as necessary, as that soldiers and executioners of the law should be firm, resolute, and in some degree unfeeling. All that men have to do with regard to noxious brutes is to keep out of their way, and arm themselves against their attacks. But in this country we have not much room for dread. We have

[1] See Dr. Priestley's *Institutes of Natural and Revealed Religion*, Vol. i. Part I. Sect. 3.

neither lions, tigers, nor wolves to molest us. Therefore, for us to infer that men may be cruel to brutes in general, because some brutes are naturally fierce and blood-thirsty, is tantamount to saying, cruelty in Britain is no sin because there are wild tigers in India. But is their ferocity and brutality to be the standard and pattern of our humanity? And, because they have no compassion, are we to have no compassion? Because they have little or no reason, are we to have no reason? Or, are we to become as very brutes as they? However, we need not go as far as India; for even in England dogs will worry and cocks will fight; (though not so often, if we did not set them on, and prepare them for the battle.) Yet what is that to us? Are we dogs? Are we fighting cocks? Are they to be our tutors and instructors, that we appeal to them for arguments to justify and palliate our inhumanity? No. Let tigers roar, let dogs worry, and cocks fight. But it is astonishing, that *men*, who boast so much of the dignity of their nature, the superior excellence of their understandings, and the immortality of their souls (which, by the by, is a circumstance which cruel men above all others have the least reason to glory in), should disgrace their dignity and understandings by recurring to the practice of the low and confessedly irrational part of the creation in vindication of their own conduct. There may be some cases indeed in which we may receive instruction from them; and there may be cases too, in which a wise man may learn instruction from a fool; but it is not therefore necessary that a wise man should too implicitly and at all times follow the apostle's rule *to become a fool that he may be wise* (1 Cor. iii. 18); nor is it necessary that a man should transform himself into a beast, to learn the behaviour becoming a man. Whatever is good deserves our imitation whether it be an ass or a pismire.[1] *Go to the ant, thou sluggard,* says Solomon. *Consider her ways and be wise.* (Prov. vi. 6.) But if a man's capacity is not so exalted as that of a pismire, or

[1] An ant. R.D.R.

if he is become stupid and obstinate, then send him for instruction to an ox or an ass; for it is thus that Israel was reproved for ignorance and ingratitude: *The ox knoweth his owner, and the ass his master's crib, but Israel doth not know, my people doth not consider.*[1] (Isa. i. 3.) There are some cases, therefore, in which we might do well to imitate them. But when we make the ferocity of savage brutes the model for our imitation, when we pay them the compliment to copy their manners in that which is most detestable, and which we naturally dread and avoid, we carry the matter too far; we betray the weakness of our own understanding; we degrade ourselves from the rank we hold as men; and with all our pretended boast of honour, the observation of David, king of Israel, is as true as it is plain: *Man that is in honour, and understandeth not, is like the beasts that perish.* (Ps. xlix. 20.)

But let us have done with trifling objections, and brutish examples, whether of real brutes, or of brutes in the shape of men. My appeal is not to brutality, nor to brutal inhumanity. And my arguments are not deduced from the natural fierceness or irrationality of the one, nor from the unnatural barbarity, blind rage, or unfeeling avarice of the other. It has been my endeavour to plead the cause of the dumb creatures on the principles of natural religion, justice, honour, and humanity. And I shall be happy if any thing which I have hitherto suggested may have the blessed effect of mollifying a single human heart; though, at the same time, I am aware of the obloquy to which every man must expose himself who presumes to encounter prejudice and long received customs. To make a comparison between a man and a brute is abominable; to talk of a man's duty to his horse or his ox is absurd; to suppose it a sin to chase a stag, to hunt a fox or

[1] There is a similar kind of reproof to the same people in the prophet Jeremiah, ch. viii. ver. 7. *The stork in the heaven knoweth her appointed times; and the turtle, and the crane, and the swallow observe the time of their coming: but my people know not the judgement of the Lord.* H.P.

course a hare is *unpolite*; to esteem it *barbarous* to throw at a cock,[1] to bait a bull, to roast a lobster or to crimp a fish is *ridiculous*. Reflections of this kind must be expected; though I have avoided as much as I could the pointing out any particular instances of cruelty; for I had rather the proposition should be general, that cruelty in any shape is foolish and detestable. But if it is applicable to any of the above mentioned particulars, I have no objection to the inference. And I will not deny that I had these, and many more than these, in view. I cannot, I dare not, give up a true and useful proposition, because the conclusion may carry in it the appearance of censure or disapprobation of the false notions or wrong practices of other men. There are some truths which ought not to be concealed. And there are some cases, and, indeed, many cases, in which, through the fear of offending, and a desire to please and recommend ourselves to favour, we carry our complaisance much too far. I would not willingly give any one offence, but, in the present case, to be silent would be cruelty, and an offence to the brutes for whose sake I write. Let it be deemed, then, in the estimation of the vulgar,[2] abominable, absurd, unpolite, or ridiculous, I am not ashamed as a Christian to testify my utter abhorrence of every instance of cruelty; and as a Minister of Christ, I scruple not to affirm, upon the genuine principles of our holy religion, that an unmerciful Christian must be either extremely ignorant of his duty, or extremely obstinate, hard-hearted, and ungrateful.

To vindicate and support this assertion, as well as to illustrate and confirm what has been before advanced on the principles of nature, I shall now appeal to the authoritative word of the great God, the benevolent Creator, and to the gospel of the blessed Jesus the

[1] Throwing sticks and other missiles at tethered poultry was still a popular pastime in eighteenth-century England, helping to give the country the reputation for being the most cruel in Europe. R.D.R

[2] By the *vulgar*, I mean the obstinate, the hard-hearted, and the ignorant, of every class and denomination. H.P.

merciful redeemer of the world. And, if it shall appear from the testimonies and examples, and from the precepts and promises contained in Holy Scripture, that mercy to brutes is a duty commanded, and that cruelty to them is a sin forbidden, then, let all objections vanish, let all the Earth keep silence before God. And though *there are many devices in a man's heart, nevertheless the counsel of the Lord, that shall stand;*[1] and every device and attempt to invalidate the duty of mercy, or to exculpate the sin of cruelty (beside its repugnance to reason and common sense), must be considered in a religious view, as taking its rise either from blindness of heart, or from pride, vain-glory and hypocrisy; or from envy, hatred and malice and all uncharitableness; or from hardness of heart and contempt of God's word and commandment.

[1] Prov. xix. 21.

CHAPTER TWO

THE first account of brute animals in Holy Scripture is in the history of the creation recorded by Moses, in the first chapter of the book intituled Genesis, or Generation: *God said, let the waters bring forth abundantly the moving creature that hath life* (or as it is in the Hebrew, and in the margin of our Bible, the moving creature that hath soul) *and fowl that may fly above the Earth in the open firmament of heaven. And God said, let the earth bring forth the living creature after his (or its) kind, cattle and creeping thing, and beast of the Earth after his kind; and it was so.* (ver. 20. and 24.)

There is a peculiar sublimity of style throughout this chapter, in which the sacred historian represents the word or mandate of the Almighty as preceding every event of creation. God said, *let be.* A form of expression this, which cannot fail to engage the attention of the reader; and it seems intended to denote that it was as easy to the supreme being to do as to speak, yet not so as to exclude the idea of the actual exertion of the divine power mediately or immediately.

Light or fire, firmament or air, water and earth, were elements of *immediate* creation, or effects of which the divine power was the sole and immediate cause.

The sun and stars, the sea and vegetables were mediate effects, or formations produced by the confluence and configurations of the elements which were before created.

But animals, or beings with life and sense, are to be considered both as productions and creations; *productions*, as to the substance or matter, and *creations*, as to life and sense.

Light or fire collected into orbs, and set in proper

places in the great expanse, became sun and stars. The waters, endued with gravity and lubricity, were gathered together, that is, ran down into the basin prepared for their reception, and so formed the sea. And the Earth, endued with the wonderful quality of vegetation, was, in the hand of its Maker, the powerful medium of the germination of grass, herbs, and trees. Yet, after all, these effects were as inanimate as the elements of which they were formed. There is something in our ideas of life and sensation, which cannot be accounted for as the mere effect of any configuration or modification of inanimate matter. The waters by confluence might hew out a rock or shape out an island; and a portion of Earth might be concreted into a precious stone or a mineral; yet rocks and islands, precious stones and minerals, are as void of sense or self-motion as if they had never been formed. Neither water nor earth (though powerful mediums to cause surprising effects), can any more communicate life and sense to their own productions, than a weight or spring can communicate life or sense to a clock or a watch. If, by the motion of the waters, the slime or substance in the bed of the sea had been thrown into the form of the most perfect fish; or if the Earth had brought forth a vegetable in the perfect form of a beast, the fish would have been lifeless as a rock or a sponge, and the beast as insensible as a stone or a blade of grass. Or, if all the elements together, by an accidental concourse, had formed beings of the shapes of all the animals that exist in the universe, and of the same substance and texture as to every part of them within and without, still they would have been but as figures of paste, or as dead corpses without life or sense.

To communicate sense to inanimate matter, or to kindle but the first spark of life (however, when so kindled or communicated to any being, that being might be enabled to continue and extend the flame to others of its own species and generation), was a new and distinct exertion of the divine agency; or it was as much a creation as the original creation of the inanimate elements; and as such it is represented to us by Moses. For though it is written, *God said, let the waters bring forth abundantly the moving creature that hath life, and fowl that may fly above the Earth in the open firmament of heaven,*[1] yet we are not to suppose, from this form of expression, that the fishes and fowls were the spontaneous generation, or the mere production of the waters without the interposition and operation of the divine power; for it follows in the next verse, *and God created great whales, and every living creature that moveth, which the waters brought forth abundantly after their kind, and every winged fowl after his kind.* The waters brought them forth, and yet God created them. That is, they were both productions and creations. And the meaning seems to be this: of the slime or mud or other necessary ingredients brought forth or yielded from the waters and earth,[2] God took thereof, and formed the fishes and fowls, and created them animals or moving creatures, by communicating to them life or soul. And God saw that they were good, good in their kind, and well adapted to their proper elements; and God blessed them.

Again *God said, let the earth bring forth the living creature after his kind, cattle, and creeping thing, and beast of the Earth after his kind; and it was so;* (ver. 24.) that is, it was so that the Earth brought forth or yielded substance or matter for the divine hand to work upon, and for the spirit of life to quicken and animate; for we read in the next verse, that *God made the beast of the Earth after his kind, and cattle after their kind; and every thing that creepeth upon the Earth after his kind.* The Earth brought forth the substances; but God shaped them and gave them life, and so made them to be animals or living creatures. And God saw that they were good.

[1] Gen. i. 20.
[2] That earth as well as water was part of the substance of fowls is evident from ch. ii. 19, and therefore it is most likely it was part of the substance of fishes, though the writer does not mention them in that place, because the fishes were not brought to Adam. H.P.

THE DUTY OF MERCY

From this account of the creation it plainly appears that the fishes of the sea, and every creature that moveth in the waters; the fowls of the firmament, and every creature that flieth in the air; the wild beasts of the Earth, and the tame cattle of the Earth, and every thing that creepeth upon the Earth; all and every brute animal, from the great whale to the creeping worm, were made and created by the divine appointment, and by the operation and power of that God who in the beginning created the heaven and the Earth.

I observed above, that every animal was a *creation* as well as a *production*. And this is no less true of Man (the last made and created, but the most perfect and most eminent of all the terrestrial animals) than it is of brutes. For we read: *The Lord God formed man of the dust of the ground, and breathed into his nostrils the breath of life, and Man became a living soul* (ch. ii. ver. 7.)

Distinguished and exalted as man is above all the other animals, there is nothing recorded of him as to his origin that is not applicable to them likewise. *The Lord God formed man of the dust of the ground.* And the same is said of the beasts and birds: *Out of the ground the Lord God formed every beast of the field, and every fowl of the air* (ch. ii. 19.) As to substance, then, men and brutes are alike *of the dust of the ground*. And to the same purpose, saith the Royal Preacher, speaking of men and beasts, *all are of the dust, and all turn to dust again* (Eccl. iii. 20.). The truth of the last part of the sentence is indisputable, that all turn to dust; and daily experience demonstrates it. Therefore we have reason to conclude that the former is equally true, and all are *of* the dust. And this is confirmed to us by the declaration of God unto Adam: *Thou shalt return unto the ground; for out of it wast thou taken; for dust thou art, and unto dust shalt thou return* (Gen. iii. 19.).

It is further said of man, *and God breathed into his nostrils the breath of life*. If we turn to the sixth and seventh chapters, we find the words *Breath of Life* applied both to brutes and to men. For when God declared to Noah that *he would bring a flood of waters upon the Earth, to destroy all flesh, wherein is the breath of life* (ch. vi. 7.), it appears throughout the seventh chapter, that the brutes are included in the words *flesh, wherein is breath of life*. And the brutes that were saved, are described in the same form of words: They, Noah and his family, *and every beast ... and all the cattle ... and every creeping thing ... and every fowl ... and every bird went in unto Noah into the ark, two and two of all flesh, wherein is the breath of life* (ch. vii. 14.). And more particularly, more expressly, and remarkably in verses 21, 22: *All flesh died, that moved upon the Earth, both of fowl, and of cattle, and of beast, and of every creeping thing that creepeth upon the earth ... all in whose nostrils was the breath of life, of all that was in the dry land,*[1] died. The brutes then have the breath of life in their nostrils, as well as men. *The God that made the world and all things therein* (said St. Paul to the Athenians, Acts xvii. 25.), *giveth to all life and breath*. And when *He taketh away their breath, they die, and return to their dust* (Ps. civ. 29.). *And that which befalleth the sons of men*, says Solomon (Eccles. iii. 19.), *befalleth beasts; as the one dieth, so dieth the other; yea, they have all one breath; so that a man* (in this respect) *hath no pre-eminence above a beast.. All go unto one place; all are of the dust; and all return to dust again*. He then subjoineth this very pertinent question, *Who knoweth the spirit of a man that goeth upward, and the spirit of a beast that goeth downward to the Earth?* As much as to say, who knoweth the difference (as to this world) between a man and a beast? Or wherein has a man any pre-eminence above a beast, except that a man walketh erect, and so *his breath goeth upward*, but a beast walketh prone,[2] and so *his breath goeth down-*

---

[1] The limitation in this place, *of all that were on the dry land*, intimates that the fishes, though not on the dry land, were creatures *in whose nostrils was the breath of life*. H.P.

[2] Pronaque cum spectent animalia cætera terram; / Os homini sublime dedit: coelumque tueri / Jussit, et erectos ad sidera tollere vultus. / OVID, Metamorphoses.

THE DUTY OF MERCY

ward to the Earth? I confess this comparison, and this home [*sic*] question, is very humiliating; but I desire it may be observed, that I quote the words of Holy Scripture, which seems to represent men and brutes in their original constitution as nothing more than breathing dust.

But it is added in the creation of man, that man became a living soul. *The Lord God formed man of the dust of the ground, and breathed into his nostril the breath of life; and man became a living soul.*[1] Now, if man became a living soul by God's breathing into his nostrils the breath of life, every creature into whose nostrils was breathed the breath of life became a living soul likewise. But we have seen above that all the creatures who perished in the flood were such in whose nostrils was the breath of life;[2] therefore, all those creatures, whether fowls or cattle, or beasts, or creeping things, were living souls; and consequently all of the same kind, at this day, are living souls. And such they are in Hebrew scripture said to be; and so they are denominated in our English bibles according to the margin, which has been always understood as of the same authority as the context itself. Thus, *let the waters bring forth the moving creature that hath life*: in the Hebrew, and in the margin, *that hath soul* (ch. i. 20.). And, *to every beast of the earth, and to every fowl of the air, and to every thing that creepeth upon the earth, wherein there is life*: in the Hebrew, and in the margin, *wherein there is a living soul* (ver. 30.).

The sum of the whole is this. In the scripture account of the original constitution of men and brutes, the very same terms are applied to both. Are the brutes of the dust of the ground? So is man. Have men the breath of life in their nostrils? So have brutes. Are the one living souls? So are the other. For *the Lord God formed both man and brute of the dust of the ground, and breathed into their nostrils the breath of life, and so man and*

[1] Gen. ii. 7.
[2] Gen. vii. 22.

brute became living souls, or living substances (ch. vii. 4. 23.)

I hope I shall not be misunderstood in this short disquisition concerning the creation of brute animals, as if I meant hereby in any respect to disparage the real dignity and excellence of mankind. I acknowledge with all thankfulness and humility that there are perfections, endowments, and advantages on the side of men, which elevate us far above the brutes; and when we take into the account the future immortality of man, the distance between us is infinite. But as it appeared to me necessary, in a treatise of this nature, to consider the origin of the creatures who are the subjects of it, it would have been an act of great partiality to ourselves, and of injustice to their cause, to have omitted any circumstance that may be advanced in their favour, to conciliate some attention from us towards them. And surely it is something in their favour, when, *in looking to the rock from whence Adam was hewn, and to the hole of the pit from whence he was digged,*[1] we find that, in our original composition, we are all *of the dust of the ground*, that we are all *of one breath*, that *we have all one Father*, and that *one God created us*.

In dominion, rationality and future immortality, a man hath undoubtedly the preference to a brute; and in these respects he is *made in the image, after the likeness of God.*[2] But let it be observed that he is but a created image, or an image of appointment. It is not absolutely necessary to his constitution as a living creature, that he should be thus appointed and distinguished. He might have been without dominion, without reason and without immortality; and yet would have been a man as to figure, feature, nakedness and upright posture.

Dominion is a gift[3] or grant unto man, for which he is

---

[1] Isa. li. 1.
[2] Gen. i. 26.
[3] *Thou madest him to have dominion over the works of thy hands.* Ps. viii. 6.

THE DUTY OF MERCY

accountable to Him that gave and granted it; and which may, and in some cases has, been taken away from a man without his ceasing to be a man. And whenever he abuses the power and *dominion* which God has given him *over the fish of the sea, and over the fowl of the air, and over the cattle, and over all the Earth, and over every creeping thing that creepeth upon the Earth;*[1] whenever he tyrannizes over them with the brutal fierceness of a shark, a vulture, or a tiger, though he may retain the shape of a man, he degenerates into a monster, and forfeits the title of the image of God, whose mercies are over all his works.

And as dominion, so *reason* is a gift unto man, yet not inseparable from the human form, as is evident in the case of idiots. And whenever we abuse that reason, and act beneath the character and dignity of a rational creature, we lose the divine image in that respect; we have nothing to denominate us men but outward shape; or, in other words, we become brutes in the shapes of men.

And, as dominion and reason, so future *immortality* is a gift;[2] and, being a gift, we have a natural claim or right to it, but by the grace of the donor. We cannot claim it merely because we are *animated dust*; for on this pretence a lion may put in the very same claim. Nor can we claim it through any merit of our own; for *it is God that worketh in us both to will and to do;*[3] or, God gave us our powers of thinking and acting. If it should be said that we are entitled to it through the merit of another, it is plain that, exclusive of that merit, we should have no claim to it at all. Or if it should be said that, from the first moment of our existence, immortality was stamped upon us, or that God created *Man to be immortal, and made him to be an image of his own eternity,*[4] still it was

---

[1] Gen. i. 26.
[2] *The gift of God is eternal life through Jesus Christ our lord.* Roman vi. 23.
[3] Phil. ii. 13.
[4] Wisd. ii. 23.

God's will and pleasure thus to dignify and distinguish the dust of the ground in one shape, from the like dust of the ground in another shape. *It was God that made thee to differ from a brute; and what hast thou, that thou didst not receive?* (1 Cor. iv. 7.).

Great, then, as man is, rational and immortal, image and likeness of God; how exalted soever his station now, or whatever it may be hereafter, it invalidates not this truth, that our difference from and excellence above the brutes is through the gift and grace of God. In the first point of existence, in our original composition, we seem to have been more upon a level; and during our existence here, we subsist together as the joint and temporary tenants of the earth, alike as to passion, sense and appetite; and alike subject to infirmity, pain and death. The brutes eat, and drink, and see, and hear, and taste, and smell and have organs of sensation as well as men. The blood circulates in their veins as in our own. They hunger, they thirst, they faint for want of food and refreshment; and man hath the same passions, and stands in need of the same support. And when God *taketh away their breath, they die, and return to their dust* (Ps. civ. 29.). And when *the breath of man goeth forth, he returneth to his earth* (Ps. cxlvi. 4.). In some respects – in strength, in swiftness, in scent and sharp-sightedness - it is certain that many of them exceed us. And though it is true in general that the brutes have neither shape nor the reason of men, yet it is likewise true, that some brutes approach so *near* to the human shape, and some men seem to be so *defective* as to reason, that upon comparison . . .

But comparisons are odious. We will suppose man, in all respects, and at all times, so perfect and so distinguished, that no comparison can, or ought to be made. Yet thus much, I presume, will be granted, that a brute is a creature superior to a stone, and that some of them possess properties and qualities which are not unworthy of the notice and attention of men, in as much as they tend to display the power and wisdom of their great creator.

THE DUTY OF MERCY

I will fetch my knowledge from afar, said Elihu to Job, *and will ascribe righteousness to my Maker. Behold, God is mighty, and despiseth not any; he is mighty in strength and wisdom.* (chap. xxxvi. 3-5). *Hearken unto this, O Job; stand still, and consider the wondrous works of God.* (Chap. xxxvii. 14). The mighty *is excellent in power*. (Ver. 23). But how shall Job consider this? Or from whom shall he learn instruction? For, in the extremity of his grief, he had said *to corruption, thou art my father; and to the worm, thou art my mother and my sister*;[1] and to the like purpose had Bildad said: *man is a worm, and the son of man is a worm*.[2] To evince, therefore, the excellence of the divine power, the sublime writer of this noble and incomparable poem, as if he thought it beyond human description, introduces the Almighty as in a whirlwind, condescending to expostulate with Job upon the subject;[3] first, by an appeal to the *ordinances of heaven*,[4] directed and controlled by the over-ruling power and appointment of God; and then, by referring him to the living tokens and effects of more than human power and greatness, manifested in the prodigious strength, or amazing swiftness, or graceful beauty, or enormous stature, or tremendous fierceness of the most eminent of the brute creatures; and particularly exemplified in the lion, the raven, the wild goat, the hind, the wild ass, the unicorn, the peacock, the ostrich, the horse, the hawk, the eagle, the behemoth or elephant and the leviathan[5] or crocodile (Ch. xxxviii. xxxix. xl. xli.)

---

[1] Ch. xvii. 14., [2] Ch. xxv. 6.
[3] *The whole speech for sublimity of style and matter is worthy of the divine majesty, and so far above being equalled by any human composition, that I am satisfied no one can have the vanity to attempt it.* Worthington's Dissertation on the Book of Job, at the end of *The Essay on Redemption*, page 525. H.P.
[4] Ch. xxxviii. 33.
[5] The description of the *Leviathan* in ch. xli. induces me to think that this creature is the *crocodile*, and not the *whale*, as some have supposed. It was the great *dragon* of the rivers, and more known in Egypt, where Moses was educated, than the whale. See Ps. lxxiv. 13, 14. Isa. xxvii. 1. Ezech. xxix. 3. and xxxii. 2. H.P.

AND SIN OF CRUELTY TO BRUTE ANIMALS

These noble brutes, in a most remarkable manner, and indeed every living creature in some respect or other, do so evidently declare the wisdom and power of God, that the Royal Psalmist calls upon them all, from the greatest to the smallest, to join in the grand chorus to the praise of the great Creator: *Praise the Lord from the Earth, ye dragons, and all* ye creatures in the depths of the sea; ye *beasts and all cattle, creeping things and flying fowl, praise ye the Lord* (Ps. cxlviii. 7, 10, 14). And *let everything that hath breath praise the Lord* (Ps. cl. 6.).

CHAPTER THREE

FROM the consideration of God's power exhibited in the creation of the brute animals, let us now proceed to the contemplation of his goodness manifested in his providence over them.

The Lord of the heavens and Earth, the creator of the waters is the king of every creature.[1] What God hath created he cannot but love, and what he loveth cannot but be the object of his goodness. *O Lord, thou lovest all the things that are* (saith the writer of the excellent but too much neglected book of Wisdom,[2]) *and abhorrest nothing that thou has made; for never wouldst thou have made any thing, if thou hadst hated it. And how could any thing have endured, if it had not been thy will? Or been preserved, if not called by thee?*

No creature, that God hath made, can be unknown to or disregarded by him. Hear the words of the great Creator himself, who in the fiftieth Psalm is represented as the speaker in terms that command our utmost attention: *The mighty God, even the Lord, hath spoken, and called to the Earth from the rising of the sun unto the going down thereof; every beast of the forest is mine, and the cattle upon a thousand hills; I know all the fowls of the mountains, and the wild beasts of the field are mine; or with me;*[3] *or in my sight;*[4] i.e. of my creation and under my protection.

The goodness and the mercy of God are as extensive as his wisdom and power. For what he hath created by

---

[1] Judith ix. 12.
[2] Wisdom of Solomon, xi. 24, 25.
[3] The margin
[4] *Common Prayer* version.

his power and wisdom, he preserveth by his goodness and mercy. *The eyes of all wait upon thee, O Lord, and thou givest them their meat in due season. Thou openest thine hand and satisfiest the desire of every living thing.*[1] No sooner were the animals created than they received the blessing of their creator. For having appointed unto man his proper food, and declared what should be meat for him,[2] he then adds, as a testimony of his providential care over the brutes: *to every beast of the Earth, and to every fowl of the air, and to every thing that creepeth upon the Earth, wherein there is life, I have given every green herb for meat.* (Gen. i. 30).

How excellent is thy loving-kindness, O God; thou preservest man and beast (Ps. xxxvi. 6). *O give thanks unto the God of heaven, who giveth food to all flesh: for his mercy endureth for ever* (Ps. cxxxvi. 25).

But beside these declarations in Holy Scripture concerning the benevolence of God to all his creatures in general, let us turn to the CIVth Psalm, and we shall find therein a strikingly beautiful illustration of his providential goodness to various species of them. Which psalm, if any man can read deliberately, without some tender emotion, he must be either very proud of himself, or very insensible of the divine goodness and greatness. *Bless the Lord, O my Soul; for he sendeth the springs into the valleys which run amongst the hills;* and why? That *all the beasts of the field may drink thereof; and the wild asses quench their thirst;* and that *the fowls of the air may have their habitation* in the trees nourished by their moisture, and sing and chirp among the branches. *He watereth the hills from his chambers above;* and *the Earth is satisfied with the fruit of his works;* and why? Because *it brings forth grass for the cattle,* as well as *herb for the service of man. The trees*

---

[1] Ps. cxlv. 15, 16.
[2] Gen. i. 29.

of the Lord are full,[1] *even the tall cedars of libanus which he hath planted.*[2] To what purpose? Only to please the eye of man, or to afford him timber for his house and a shelter from the storm? The psalmist assigns another reason: *that the birds might there make their nests; and as for the stork, the fir trees are her house.* Let us next survey the high hills, and the craggy mountains and rocks inaccessible to men, and dangerous for us to climb; yet they are not without use, or inhabitant; for *the high hills are a refuge for the wild goats; and the stony rocks* are a retreat and habitation *for the conies,* a weak and timorous race of animals which could hardly be safe in more frequented places; and concerning whom Agur in the book of Proverbs[3] makes the like observation, that as they are but *a feeble folk, they make their houses in the rocks.* The psalmist then proceeds to contemplate the good providence of God both to man and beast, in appointing *the darkness of the night,* as the most convenient season, for *the wild beasts of the forest to move and creep forth,* when they can be the least obnoxious unto men; for then *do the lions roar after their prey, and seek their meat from God.* And having fulfilled their pleasure and appointed task in devouring the dead bodies of animals, which, for want of such scavengers, would probably infect the air and render it offensive and unwholesome; when *the sun ariseth, they get away together, and lay them down in their dens,* that they may be no obstruction to the industrious man, *who goeth forth in safety to his work and to his labour, until the evening,* when the wild beasts sally forth again. Struck with a just sense and

---

[1] In both our translations it is rendered *full of sap,* but I have here omitted *of sap,* because it is not in the *Hebrew.* The word IShBOU denotes *fulness* in general; and in its extent it means not only *fulness of sap,* but likewise fulness as to *growth, height, leaves, fruits and branches,* and whatever might contribute to render the trees more useful and convenient to their inhabitants. H.P.
[2] Those trees are said to be *the trees of the Lord and planted by him,* which grow of themselves, without the art and care of men. H.P.
[3] Prov. xxx. 26.

reverential awe of the wisdom and goodness of the great Creator, the enraptured psalmist cannot refrain from bursting out in accents of love and admiration: *O Lord, how manifold are they works; in wisdom hast thou made them all: the Earth is full of thy riches. And, not only the Earth and air, but so also is the great and wide sea, where the leviathan taketh his pastime, and wherein are things moving innumerable, both small and great living creatures.*[1] *These wait all upon thee, that thou mayest give them their meat in due season. Thou givest them, they gather; thou openest thine hand, they are filled with good.* Thus sung the *sweet psalmist of Israel*[2] in hymns of praise unto the Lord his God, who, though *clothed with majesty and honour, and high above all nations, and his glory above the heavens, yet humbleth himself to behold the things that are in heaven and earth.*[3]

The goodness and benevolence of God to the brute creatures seem to have made such an impression upon the mind of David, and to have been so favourite a theme with him, and he takes such frequent occasions to introduce their names into his most sacred poems and most ardent prayers, that one would almost suppose he thought to render God the more propitious towards men, by reminding him, as it were, of his mercy, and loving kindness to creatures so much inferior to men. When he was bewailing his own misery and weakness, he compares himself to the lowest reptile: *I am a worm, and no man* (Ps. xxii. 6.). When he was interceding for his people in the time of plague, he recommends them to the divine mercy and forbearance, under the denomination of harmless and inno-

---

[1] As *beast* in our language denotes a *land* animal, and the subjects in this place are *water* animals, I have substituted *living creatures* for *beasts*. And thus the Hebrew word ChIUT is rendered in Ezek. i. 5. H.P.
[2] 2 Sam. xxiii. 1.
[3] Ps. cxiii. 6.

cent sheep:[1] *I it is that have sinned and done evil indeed; but as for these sheep, what have they done?* (1 Chron. xxi. 17). And when deprived of the opportunity of attending the public worship; when his mind was contemplating the *amiableness of God's tabernacle;* when his *soul was longing and fainting for the courts of the Lord, and his very heart and flesh crying out for the living God,* the sparrow and the swallow are the mediators of his supplication: *The sparrow hath found an house, and the swallow a nest for herself, where she may lay her young, even thine altars, O Lord of hosts, my king and my God* (Ps. lxxxiv. 3).

In the CXLVIIth Psalm, he calls for the harp to accompany the voice of melody: *O sing unto the Lord with thanksgiving, sing praises upon the harp unto our God; who covereth the heaven with clouds, and prepareth rain for the Earth, and maketh the grass to grow upon the mountains.*[2] *He giveth to the beast his food, and feedeth the young ravens which cry or call upon him.* With God no creature is contemptible. By his general providence he hath manifested his love and his tenderness towards all. Even a young raven cannot call upon him, but the Lord will hear its cry and will answer it: *for he provideth for the raven his food, when his young ones cry unto God* (Job xxxviii. 41).

It is not improbable that our Lord Jesus had an eye to the last mentioned passages of scripture, when he commanded his disciples to *consider the ravens, which neither sow nor reap, neither have storehouse nor barn, for God feedeth them* (Luke xii. 24). In another place this sentiment is expressed in more general terms: *Behold the fowls of the air, they sow not, neither do they reap, nor gather into barns, yet your heavenly father feedeth*

---

[1] It is well known that our blessed Saviour frequently calls the members of his church his sheep, which word likewise occurs in the daily liturgy of the Church of England. *We have erred and strayed – like lost sheep.* H.P.

[2] In the *Common Prayer Book* version, it is added, *and herb for the use of men*; but as this is not in the Hebrew, nor in our Bible version, I omit it in this place. H.P.

THE DUTY OF MERCY

them (Matt. vi. 25). That same God, to whom you are to address yourselves by the endearing, and yet exalted title of *our Father which art in heaven*, and to whom you are daily to put up this petition of dependence, *give us this day our daily bread*, that *heavenly Father*, that giver of bread, who daily feedeth you, *feedeth also the ravens and the fowls of the air.*

It was a usual method of teaching with our blessed Saviour, to deduce his arguments from nature and common observation; and, particularly, when it was his design, either to correct the pride, or to mollify the hearts of his hearers. When he would remonstrate with the people, whom he came to redeem, concerning their perverseness and ingratitude towards him, and his tender affection and concern for them, he borrows a simile from the circumstance of *a hen that would have gathered together her chickens under her wings, but they would not.*[1] And when he would convince his disciples of the providence and love of God towards men, and of the duty of trust and confidence in him, he refers them to the sparrows; as to beauty and melody the most inferior of all the feathered race; and held so cheap with men, that two of them are worth but one farthing, yet not so cheap in the estimation of the God that created them as to be beneath his notice, or unworthy of his care. *Are not two sparrows sold for a farthing? And one of them shall not fall to the ground without your Father* (Matt. x. 29). And that our Lord did not mean hereby barely to represent to his disciples the extensive knowledge of the Creator, exclusive of his providential care and tenderness towards them, is evident from another passage in which he expresses himself more particularly: *Are not five sparrows sold for two farthings? And not one of them is forgotten before God* (Luke xii. 6). Whether two sparrows for one farthing, or (which is cheaper still) five sparrows for two farthings, not one of them shall fall to the ground without your father; not one of them is forgotten before God.

---

[1] Matt. xxiii. 37. Luke xiii. 34, quoted from 2 Esdras, i. 30.

Now, to what purpose these numerous testimonies of scripture, which I have collected together in proof of the superintending care of God over all his creatures, but to enlarge the mind of man, and to teach us that, as God is the common father of the whole creation, his mercy is over all his works? "The goodness, the mercy, the kindness, the love of God towards his creatures, is so clearly laid down in express words, throughout the scriptures, that the greatest caution should always be taken not to offend against them; and no nations must ever lead us to run counter to them."[1] Not even a sparrow is forgotten before God, but holds a place in the divine remembrance. Insignificant as many of the creatures may appear to us, they are all in the sight, and under the protection of the great and merciful Creator. They are all recorded in his book; and it is he that clothes, and feeds, and preserves them. And well it is for most of them, that they are in God's keeping, and not in ours; for we show too plainly by our treatment of those animals that are in our power and are committed to our care and management, what would be the unhappy fate of all the rest if they were left to our disposal. Not that the supreme being is the less concerned for some than for others; for they are all of them parts of his great family upon Earth, though some of them are more immediate objects of his care and protection than others.

Creatures at large God claims as his own peculiar property. *All the beasts of the forest are mine*, saith the mighty God, *and so are the cattle upon a thousand hills; I know all the fowls upon the mountains, and the wild beasts of the field are in my sight.*[2] With regard to *these* creatures, he requires not our care and attention. He does not expect that we should concern or trouble ourselves about them. The duty of men concerning animals that are *wild* by nature, lies in a very narrow

---

[1] Dr. Sykes. H.P. Presumably Arthur Ashley Sykes (1684?-1756), pamphleteer and divine. R.D.R.
[2] Ps. 1. 10, 11.

compass: *let them alone.* Being God's property, and in his sight, God will provide for them. And it is enough for us that we invade not their province, but leave them unmolested and at liberty to perform the tasks, and answer the ends, for which God was pleased to create them.

Our principal duty and business is to consider the creatures of the tame and domestic kind; such as come frequently in our way, or are daily before our eyes, or are appointed to the special use and service of men, and are assigned over to our care, management and protection. Which animals, if I might be permitted to give them a particular name, to distinguish them from *brutes of ferocity,* I would denominate *brutes of humanity,* because they have not that enmity or natural aversion to mankind, which is discernible in the rest of the brutes.

It is an instance of the wisdom and goodness of God, that the brutes should be animals irrational and dumb. As to brutes of ferocity, it is certain, that if, beside their strength, swiftness and sharpness of tooth or talon, they were endued with the powers of reason and speech, men, who are animals naturally defenceless, and comparatively slow of motion, would live in perpetual fear and dread of them. And with regard to brutes of humanity, particularly the large and laborious kind, were they capable of reason, the reflection upon their subordinate and servile condition would render them very unhappy in themselves; and perhaps less tractable, and consequently less useful to us. And if to the power of reason, we suppose them likewise endued with the power of speech, the inconvenience to men would be much greater. For these brutes, by the united faculties of reason and speech, would be able to enter into combinations and conspiracies against mankind. Nor need we doubt but that this, in fact, would frequently be the case. By their constant intercourse with men, they would soon discover our natural weakness, and their own stature and strength; and the sense of their hard slavery, and of the injurious treatment they meet with from us, would probably awaken their resentment to a general insurrection, if not to the total throwing off of the human yoke. It is, therefore, a peculiar advantage to men, that the brutes have not the faculties of reason and speech.

It is a further proof of the goodness and providence of God, that the large brutes of humanity, whose great strength and stature we are so much indebted to for labour and draught, should be so remarkably *tractable* and *tame*. For if, with their strength and stature, they had that savageness and ferocity of heart, or that aversion or enmity to mankind, which many other large brutes have, they would be too formidable for our use; and we should as submissively bow down before their magnanimity and power, as we now insult over their timidity and inoffensiveness.

For our service, God has been pleased to create these useful animals large and strong; and for our security it is, that they are timid, irrational and dumb. But, certainly, it does not become us to take a cruel advantage of any of their incapacities or defects, which are only intended as the reins by which we are to guide and control them. They are tendered to us with strength sufficient for labour; but with hearts humbled, and mollified, and willing to submit to the delightful and noble service of being useful unto men. And happy are they, when they find we accept their willing obedience, by our kind and tender usage of them. They are entirely in our power, and committed to our care. And it is not improbable that God has assigned his own providence over them to us, that they may be the more tractable, the more they find themselves dependent upon us. But then it is our duty to consider that their service to us, and dependence upon us, and their own natural incapacities, lay a kind of claim and demand upon our attention and tenderness. There is a condition and restriction implied in the compact. And as all delegated dominion is founded on general utility, the power granted unto men to rule over the brutes, cannot be a power to abuse or oppress them.

It is the perfection of a wise and good government not

to take away the necessary distinctions of its subjects, nor to put them all upon an equality, but to consult and provide for the happiness of every individual according to his respective station. Therefore, the wise and good lawgiver of the universe, the king of every creature, extends his care and concern to every subject in his vast dominion. To the service of men he tenders animals of various kinds, to help our weaknesses, and to supply our wants. And to preserve due subordination, he has thought it good to deny these animals those faculties of reason and speech, with which he has been pleased to bless and distinguish mankind. Yet ungrateful man, with all his reason unreasonable, deaf to the voice of justice, and obdurate to the feelings of compassion, abuses his power and dominion over these poor creatures; because, for his sake, they are defenceless, irrational, and dumb; because they are unable to resist us, and have neither argument to convince us of our injustice, nor speech to utter their complaints.

But though man be cruel and unjust, the Lord is righteous and merciful. The defects and necessities of brutes of humanity plead hard for pity and support. And the less they are able to vindicate themselves against the abuse of human power, the more they stand in need of superior interposition on their behalf. Though beneath the notice of men, they are not beneath the notice of the God that made them. His mercies are over all his works. To check the swellings of our pride, to prevent the abuse of our power, and to curb the impetuosity of our passion and malice, he graciously condescends to reason and to speak for those, who cannot reason and speak for themselves. He not only pleads the cause of all his creatures in general, by the testimonies of his own goodness and mercy towards all, observable by the light of nature, or recorded in his holy word; but he has likewise been pleased to give particular laws, by precept or by example, for the regulation of our conduct towards those brutes who are more immediately within our power; and, therefore, are most liable to suffer by the abuse of it. What these particular laws are, I purpose now to consider. But I shall first beg leave to make a short observation, which I recommend to, and hope is not unworthy of, the notice of Christians, as it is a proof that the God of the Christians is a God that delighteth in mercy. *Blessed be God, even the father of our Lord Jesus Christ, the father of mercies, and the God of all comfort* (2. Cor. i. 3).

It has been the opinion of some Christians, that the law of Moses was superseded by the Gospel of Jesus. It is not my design here to enquire whether or how far this is true. But it is with singular pleasure that I observe as to the subject of mercy, and particularly of mercy to brutes, that however God may have been pleased to vary in his dispensations towards mankind, by obliterating an old covenant to establish a new one, yet his covenant for brutes is invariably the same. He leaveth them not without witness. Whether god of the Jew or god of the Gentile, he ceaseth not to be the father of mercies and the god of all comfort. The laws of mercy and tenderness towards the brutes, enjoined in the Old Testament, he transcribeth into the New Testament (as I shall show in my procedure) and hath thereby instructed us that, notwithstanding we are the adopted sons of God by grace, we are not to forget that by nature we are of the dust of the ground, as well as the brutes; that the virtues of justice, mercy and humility, are still as essential to a Christian as they were formerly to a Jew; and that the privileges of Christianity are not intended to cancel the duties of humanity.

CHAPTER FOUR

THERE are three instances of regard, which the creatures, who are intrusted to our care, in consideration of their service, and dependence upon us, have an undoubted right to, and which, on the principles of natural religion, they may justly demand of us; and these are food, rest, and tender usage. These three demands of food, rest and tender usage, the goodness of the great God their creator has been pleased to covenant for on their behalf, and to enjoin and ratify in his written law.

I. As to the duty of giving them food in due season, it is thus commanded in the fifth book of Moses, entitled Deuteronomy, or the Repetition of the Law: *thou shalt not muzzle the ox when he treadeth out the corn* (Ch. xxv. 4). This is a precept of justice and mercy. The cattle are, upon the whole, the cheapest servants that we keep. They want neither our money nor our clothes. Gold and silver are of no more account with them than the stones of the street. And as to clothes, they are provided by nature with better and more durable garments than all the art of man can furnish them with. In this they have the advantage of us; and if they were as capable of pride as men are, they would put this endowment and array of nature into the balance, as more than a counterpoise to Solomon in all his glory. For let a man be ever so well dressed, his clothes are but the covering of his shame, and artificial supplies for natural defects. Every ornament he wears to grace his person, is a tacit acknowledgement that without that ornament he would be less beautiful and amiable; and that in himself he is so imperfect, that he stands in need of invented ornaments to set him off. And even his necessary clothes are either taken from the ground which the cattle tread under their feet, or else are borrowed skins, borrowed feathers, or borrowed hair. The creatures, which we despise, wore them before we had them, and could call them their own; whilst we are glad to be their heirs, and to wear them at second hand, when they have left them off: nor even then can we apply them to our use and service, without much contrivance and preparation. But to the brutes their clothes are suitable to their wants; they are the endowments of nature and the gifts of God. And well for them it is, that nature has, in this instance, been so bountiful and indulgent towards them; for if many of the cattle were as ill-clothed as they are too often ill-fed and hard wrought, they would be wretched creatures indeed.

Food is all the wages which the labouring brutes expect or desire, for all their toil and drudgery in the service of man; and to deny them food is not only imprudent in the master on his own account, but it is barbarous, wicked and unjust. They ask only the *Grass of your field.* I mean the grass of *the* field, for *you* have no property in nature; we are only temporary tenants, with leave to take to our use the fruits of the Earth. The soil is the property of God, the lord paramount of the manor, who hath made the grass to grow for the cattle. The grass of the field, therefore, is no gift of yours to them; it is their *right*; their property; it was provided for them, and given to them, before man was created.[1] And as man cannot eat grass, and the beast asks for that only which man cannot eat, to withhold or forbid it is a robbery and a sin. Therefore, if to gratify thine appetite or avarice, thou ploughest up one field; and to save the sweat of thine own brow, instead of digging it with a spade, makest use of the labour and strength of thy cattle to plough it for thee; in the name of gratitude and justice, forget not thy benefactors, but allow them another field, or something equivalent to it, in lieu of

---

[1] *And God said ... to every beast of the Earth ... I have given every green herb for meat.* Gen. i. 30.

that which you have taken from them. *Muzzle not the oxen that treadeth out thy corn.* Consider well, if the corn you sow and reap is *thy* corn, not their corn; the grass you dig up is *their* grass, not your grass. And when God appointed you to be master of the beast, and tenant of the field, he gave you no right to deprive your beast of that food which God hath ordained for him; but as lord of the manor he demands of you a quit-rent for the use of the beast that ploughs and labours for thee.

I know, indeed, it is unnecessary, and might seem like trifling, to endeavour to persuade, or to convince a man of the reasonableness, expediency, or advantage accruing to himself, in feeding his horse or his ox; the owner's interest will prompt him to it, without advice. The most cruel master will not starve the slave by whom he gets his bread; nay, perhaps, will give him food enough to go through his work; but this is not all that is required in the divine precept, *muzzle not the ox that treadeth out the corn.* For if food and barely food enough to support life is all that is meant by it, I presume it would not have been delivered as a sacred command. Not to *muzzle* the ox, implies something else than not to *starve* him. To starve him to death is such a mixture of folly and cruelty, that no man of common sense or common humanity can ever be supposed to be guilty of it. But to muzzle him whilst treading out the corn, or labouring for the food of man, is not unusual even with those who would be esteemed merciful. The precept, therefore, enjoins the care and attention of the master to the ease and happiness of his beast; and that he ought not to suffer the poor creature to be tantalized with the sight of what is agreeable to him, or would be a refreshment to him, and refuse to indulge his longing appetite. His labour deserves wages; and his particular labour, at the time of *treading corn*[1] for the appetite of man, should remind us that the beast has *his* appetite

---

[1] *The ox is not to be muzzled when he treads out the corn; for it would be unreasonable to deny any thing a part of the fruit of its own labours.* Josephus, *Jewish Antiquities*, Book iv. ch. 6.

likewise. The circumstance of the work itself should then make us more attentive to his wants; and the harder his task is, the more it behoves the master to alleviate his fatigue by frequent indulgences and refreshment. To suffer a beast, therefore, who is labouring for the support of our nature, and who is as sensible of hunger as we are, and yet harnessed and restrained from indulging his appetite, whilst we can gratify our own whenever we please; to suffer this useful beast to pine for his meat, is putting a muzzle to the ox that treadeth out the corn; and though this may not be called an absolute act of cruelty, yet in my opinion it has a tendency to unmercifulness and injustice.

And if so, no less unmerciful and unjust is it to withhold from the labouring beast his due quantity of drink, which is as necessary to his support and refreshment as meat, and is part of his food as well as grass or straw. The Lord *covereth the heaven with clouds*, and *prepareth rain for the Earth ... to give to the beast his food* (Ps. cxlvii. 8, 9). And *He sendeth the springs into the valleys which run among the hills ... to give drink to every beast of the field; and the wild asses quench their thirst* (Ps. civ. 10, 11). The wild asses and brutes at large can quench their thirst at every call of nature. But the tame ass, the beasts of the field, horses and oxen, for whose sake likewise the springs were sent into the valleys, being harnessed, yoked, bridled or muzzled, must wait their master's pleasure. Yet no pretence of trouble or inconvenience, no lame excuse of business, hurry, or forgetfulness can exempt the master from his bounden duty to give food to the hungry and drink to the thirsty. Even religion itself must yield to the laws of mercy: and the most sacred seasons are profaned and misemployed by the man who neglects to attend to the wants of his cattle. When our Blessed Saviour reproved the ruler of the synagogue for his superstitious notions concerning the sabbath, as if Jesus had broken the commandment by healing a diseased woman on the sabbath day, he puts this question to him: *doth not each one of you on the sabbath loose his ox or his ass from the stall, and lead him away to watering?* (Lu. xiii. 15). In which question, our Lord takes it for granted that it was their duty to lead away their cattle to watering even on the sabbath day, the day in which the cattle were to do no manner of work. Now if to loose them from the stall and to lead them away to watering was a duty on the sabbath day, or day of rest, it must be an indispensable duty to give them the refreshment of water in the days of work, and toil and sweat. And to borrow a text from the prophet Isaiah (taking the words as I find them, without examining into their occasion or connection), a blessing attends this particular instance of duty in leading them to the watering, whether to quench their thirst, or to cool their parched feet: *blessed are ye that sow beside all waters, that send forth thither the feet of the ox and the ass* (Isa. xxxii. 20).

It is recorded of Rebecca, the sister of Laban, when she went to the well to fill her pitcher, and saw the camels of Abraham, though she knew not whose camels they were, she said unto the servant that was with them, *I will draw water for thy camels until they have done drinking* (Gen. xxiv). A very laborious task for a young woman to undertake (considering that camels are very large beasts that drink water in great abundance, which is to serve them for long travel in dry deserts; and here were no fewer than ten of these great thirsty beasts to satisfy). Nevertheless, she said, *I will draw for the camels until they have done drinking*, that is, till they have drunk their fill. And she was as good to her word, for it is said *she hasted and emptied her pitcher into the trough, and ran again unto the well to draw water, and drew for all his camels.*[1] (verse 20).

[1] What a contrast to the tenderness of Rebecca is the hardheartedness of our *sporting* females, who can testify their delight in the piercing groans of the dying and more delicate stag. In minds so abominably callous, religion can have no place. Else that I am persuaded that the pious ejaculation of the King of Israel must make some impression upon them, and cause them to relent, when the innocent and injured brute is taking to soil, through the savage cruelty of those in whose sex tenderness should be nature: *As the hart panteth after the water brooks, so panteth my soul after thee, O God.* Ps. xlii. 1. H.P.

And when her brother Laban had invited the servant to come to his house, before he gave anything to the men to eat, it is expressively said that *he ungirded the camels, and gave straw and provender for the camels* (verse 32). A circumstance this of small importance, were it not an example written for our admonition, and worthy our imitation. The camels, though faint and fatigued, might not have perished if the men had eaten and refreshed themselves before notice taken of the cattle. But compassion urged him to take the first care of those creatures, who could not take care of themselves; he had regard to their happiness. Rebecca had given drink to all the camels; and the next business was to ungird and relieve them from their burdens; and then to give them provender to eat, and straw to lie down and rest themselves upon. Therefore, *he ungirded his camels and gave straw and provender for the camels*, before any refreshment was offered to the men. The necessities of the cattle engaged his first attention; and the more speedy the relief, the most conspicuous was the humanity of it. Suffer not the beast, then, that has carried you or your baggage, and for your sake has borne the burden and heat of the day, to wait long for his necessary refreshment, but allow it him in good time. For his daily labour give him his daily wages, and refresh him as oft and as soon as he is weary.

Moses gives this law with regard to day servants: *Thou shalt not defraud thy neighbour neither rob him; the wages of him that is hired, shall not abide with thee all night until the morning* (Lev. xix. 13): and again: *at his day thou shalt give him his hire, neither shall the sun go down upon it, for he is poor, and setteth his heart upon it; lest he cry against thee unto the Lord, and it be sin unto thee* (Deut. xxiv. 15). To withhold daily wages from them to whom it is daily due, who want it, and set their heart upon it is, in the account of Moses, a fraud, a robbery, a sin and a crying sin. And St. James denounces the judgments of God against those that defraud the labourer of his hire: *Go to now, ye rich men, weep and howl for your miseries that shall come upon you ... Behold, the hire of the labourers who have reaped down your fields, which is of you kept back by fraud, crieth: and the cries of them which have reaped are entered into the ears of the Lord of sabaoth* (Ch. v. 1-4). Now if it is a fraud, a robbery, a sin and a crying sin, to withhold and keep back the wages of the hireling, it must be a sin to withhold and keep back food and refreshment which is the hire and wages of the cattle; for they both alike want it, and set their hearts upon it. The reason and rule of justice is the same in both cases. The ox that draws the plough is as necessary a servant as the labourer who guides it; and they have equally a claim to indulgence and tenderness. The same law provides for both. The cries of the defrauded beast, as well as of the defrauded labourer, will enter into the ears of the Lord of hosts; for he that said, *defraud not the labourer,* said also, *muzzle not the ox.*

St. Paul was so sensible of the close connection of these two important precepts, enjoined by the same authority, and grounded upon the same principle of justice and humanity, that (in his first Epistle to Timothy) he classes them together in such a manner that it is plain he understood them both to be of equal weight and obligation, and he quotes them both as texts of holy scripture: *The scripture saith, Thou shalt not muzzle the ox that treadeth out the corn, and The labourer is worthy of his reward* (1 Tim. v. 18). The former precept the apostle likewise quotes in his first Epistle to the Corinthians, and introduces it by declaring that the precept was more than *human*, it was of *divine* authority: *say I these things as a man? Or saith not the law the same also? For it is written in the law of Moses, Thou shalt not muzzle the mouth of the ox that treadeth out the corn* (1 Cor. ix. 8, 9).

From the question immediately following these words – *doth God take care for oxen?* – some might infer that the apostle meant to set aside or weaken the precept; or that it is only to be interpreted in a figurative or typical sense. To me it appears in another light, and that the inference of the apostle is an establishment of the commandment. It was the scope of St. Paul to prove that the ministers of the gospel have a right to a maintenance, because they *labour in the word and doctrine:*[1] and to this purpose he might have laid the stress of his reasoning upon the almost similar case of the maintenance of the priests under the Jewish law (which, indeed, he notices in verse 13), but he begins with an argument of greater force and more extensive obligation, which the change of the Priesthood did not and could not cancel; an argument which, though enjoined by the law of Moses, was founded on the law of nature and acknowledged by heathens and infidels, viz., that the labouring beast had a right to support: and if the voice of nature, and of the God of nature, require and command that the cattle shall have the wages of their work, it is but reasonable that *they which wait at the altar* should be *partakers with the altar;*[2] and for the same reason, the Lord had so *ordained that they which preach the gospel, should live of the gospel.*[3] This, then, was the force of the apostle's argument, not to infringe the duties of humanity and tenderness to the brutes, but to confirm them, and thereupon to build an argument of similar nature. To suppose otherwise is to accuse the apostle of weak reasoning. It is to suppose him to lay a foundation, and then to dig it up as soon as he begins to erect his building, which would be no great credit to a *wise master builder*[4]

Upon the equity of the maxim, acknowledged by all men, that *the labourer is worthy of his reward*; and upon the positive precept of the law, that *the labouring ox should not be muzzled,* St. Paul grounds his proof that the claim of the ministry to a maintenance is both just and legal. He thought his argument so strong and evident upon this foundation, that he scruples not to compare the case of himself and his brethren to that of

[1] 1 Tim. v. 17.
[2] 1 Cor. ix. 13.
[3] Ver. 14.
[4] 1 Cor. iii. 10.

oxen ploughing in the field. Nor did he do any discredit to his ministerial character by the parallel, or produce an instance unbecoming the dignity of his subject. For his blessed master upon a matter of more extensive importance than the maintenance of the ministry, descends much lower than St. Paul has done in this instance. Our Lord Jesus, to teach his disciples the duty and security of trusting in God for protection or deliverance from trouble, might have carried their thoughts to reflect upon the interposing and overruling providence of God in the affairs and revolutions of states and empires; or might have drawn his argument from the general view of nature directed by his wisdom and love; but instead of this, he reminds them to consider the sparrows: *are not two sparrows sold for a farthing, and one of them shall not fall on the ground without your Father? ... Fear ye not therefore, ye are of more value than many sparrows.*[1] What, then, are sparrows of no value at all? The comparison itself, on which the argument is founded, shows that they are of some, though small, value. And if the similar question of St. Paul should here occur – *doth God take care for sparrows?* – yes surely, as certainly as he takes care for men, if our Saviour, who had *the words of eternal life*,[2] spoke so as to be understood. We have here, then, it seems, the judgment of Jesus, whose authority alone is sufficient, and the judgement of Paul on the authority of Moses, that *sparrows* and *oxen* are objects of the care and providence of God: but with this difference, that whilst God shows his care for oxen mediately, by recommending them to the care of men; he takes care for sparrows immediately, by providing for them himself. The meanness or apparent insignificancy of the creature, how despicable soever in the judgement of men, is no obstruction to the love of God towards it; and upon the debasement of the subject, Christ and his apostle thought most to exalt the divine goodness, and

[1] Matt. x. 29, 31.
[2] John vi. 68.

thereby to prove the love of God unto men. Show me then the Christian who denies the providence of God over the birds of the air, and I should doubt whether his faith were sufficient to support him in the day of trial. Or show me the minister of Christ, who imagines that God doth not take care for oxen, and I should think he deserved to be muzzled till he hath better learned Christ. But as our Saviour in the one case proves the providence of God over men from his providence over the birds of the air, so doth the apostle evince the reasonableness and justice of the maintenance of the ministry from his commandment of justice and mercy to the labouring man and beast of the field: *For the scripture saith, thou shalt not muzzle the ox that treadeth out the corn. And, the labourer is worthy of his reward.*[1] And again, *who planteth a vineyard and eateth not of the fruit thereof? Or, who feedeth a flock, and eateth not of the milk of the flock? Say I these things as a man? Or saith not the law the same also? For it is written in the law of Moses, thou shalt not muzzle the mouth of the ox that treadeth out the corn.*[2] The cases being similar,[3] the rule of equity is the same. And the conclusion is this; that since it is the merciful sanction of both testaments, that the ox that labours for the service of man shall not be muzzled, the laborious beast of every kind, whether ox, or horse, or ass, has a just right to every refreshment of nature. And though he may not always be at work, yet, as his whole life and strength is devoted to the service of his master, and awaits his pleasure to work or not to work at his command, the master's care and attention to him ought never to cease. Whether at work

[1] 1 Tim. v. 18.
[2] 1 Cor. ix. 7, 8, 9.
[3] The similarity of these cases explains to us the reason why men who are cruel to their cattle do generally bear hardest upon their ministers; and why they, who make no scruple to defraud their ministers of their just and legal maintenance, are generally most cruel to their cattle. The precept of the apostle seems to contain a prophecy, that cruelty and sacrilege are sins that will go hand in hand together. I beg to recommend this observation to the serious consideration of the clergy. H.P.

or not at work, he is his master's servant and dependent; and the master by the compact and indenture of the great law of natural justice is bound to support him. And if the beast cannot help himself to what he wants, it is the master's duty to supply him with it.

Be it thy care and duty, therefore, if thou art the master of a labouring brute, to observe the foregoing precepts and examples in the article of food and refreshment. When thy beast is at work for thee, *muzzle him not*.[1] When he hath carried thee or thy burden, ease him, ungird him, and give him *straw and provender*.[2] And when tied to the full crib, if it be too much trouble to thee to empty thy *pitcher into the trough*, and to *draw water* for him,[3] yet at least remember to *loose him from the stall*, and either *send him forth*,[4] or *lead him away to the watering*.[5]

But to proceed:

II. To give the cattle food, and food in due season, is but a part of our duty towards them; or but one duty amongst others. A man may feed his beast till he swells with fatness, and yet be cruel to him, if he works him above his strength, or gives him not sufficient rest. And here again the goodness of God their creator condescends to interfere on their behalf. For it is thus written in the first table of the ten commandments, established as the great rule of practice throughout the Jewish and the Christian world: *remember the sabbath day*[6] to

---

[1] Deut. xxv. 4. [2] Gen. xxiv. 32.
[3] Gen. xxiv. 20. [4] Isa. xxxii. 20.
[5] Luke xiii. 15.
[6] By the sabbath day, I mean every *seventh* day set apart as a day of rest and devotion according to the usage of different nations: and it appears to me of little moment what day of the week is set apart to this end, provided the order of *six* and the *seventh* is observed. If the Christian church had appointed *Saturday* to have been continued as the sabbath, and the State had confirmed that appointment, it would have been our duty to have observed the Saturday and not the Sunday. The very change of the day by *human* authority (for no one will say that our Lord Jesus Christ appointed the change) shows that one day is not intrinsically more holy than another, and yet that the observance of a seventh-day

keep it holy. In it thou shalt not do any work, thou, nor thy son, nor thy daughter, nor thy man servant, nor thy maid servant, nor thy cattle, nor thy stranger that is within thy gates (Exod. xx. 8, 10). This commandment is addressed to masters and fathers of families, as is evident from the pronouns, *thy* son, *thy* daughter, *thy* servant, *thy* cattle. The transgression therefore against it, whether by child, servant or beast, is the sin of the father or master; and the most punctual observation of it on the master's part is not enough, unless the design of it extends to all under his care. It is likewise a commandment of mercy, as explained by our Lord Jesus Christ: *The sabbath was made for man, and not man for the sabbath* (Mark ii. 27). That is to say, the ordinances of religion are intended for the benefit of those to whom they are enjoined. The Supreme Being stands not in need of the service of men, nor can any of our acts of devotion profit[1] him at all. It is for our sake, and for the sake of general good to his creatures, that they are instituted. The sabbath, which is an ordinance of religion, is a merciful dispensation to all that are included in the commandment: and unless the sabbath be sanctified by works of mercy and benevolence, at least if they are neglected when opportunity for them offers, the intent of it is frustrated. For these are the

sabbath, or of a sabbath every seventh day, is absolutely necessary for the sake of man and beast, and conformable to the divine commandment. I mention this, to preclude any Christian from endeavouring to evade the force of my ensuing argument taken from the Jewish law, under pretence that the day being changed, the design of the commandment is in part changed likewise; and that the letter of the law of Moses is not binding upon Christians. I grant that the letter of the law as to the particular day is not binding, but the spirit of the law, being a law of mercy, is still binding, notwithstanding our Christian liberty. For I cannot believe that our Lord Jesus who *came to fulfil all righteousness*,[†] ever meant, in any thing he said or did, to cancel one single duty of justice or mercy. H.P.

[†] Matt. iii. 15. v. 17.
[1] *Can a man be profitable unto God, as he that is wise may be profitable unto himself?* Job xxii. 2.

weightier matters of the law, which must be done and which men of employment have more leisure to do on the sabbath day, than on other days. When, therefore, the ruler of the synagogue said unto the people *with indignation*, because Jesus had done a work of mercy to a diseased woman on that day: *there are six days in which men ought to work: in them therefore come and be healed, and not on the sabbath day* (Luke xiii. 14), our Lord vouchsafes him no better a name than hypocrite for his nice distinction; and instead of recurring to the refinements of school divinity, he appeals to the plain and more certain and easy dictates of nature and common sense, and demonstrates the duty of mercy on that day from a known practice amongst themselves: *doth not each one of you on the sabbath loose his ox or his ass from the stall, and lead him away to watering?* In which question he infers one duty from another; and is so far from blaming them for this work of mercy to an ox or an ass, that he highly approves it by making it the groundwork of his own apology: and the inference and argument was so humane, so excellent, and striking, that it is said *all his adversaries were ashamed* (verse 17), or confounded. Again, when he healed a man that had the dropsy, and the Pharisees watched him, because it was the sabbath day, and Jesus put this question to them: *Which of you shall have an ass or an ox fallen into a pit, and will not straightway pull him out on the sabbath day?* (Luke xiv. 5), it follows immediately, *and they could not answer him again to these things* (verse 6): or, they tacitly submitted to the force of his reasoning. And at another time, when *there was a man* in the synagogue *which had his hand withered, and they asked Jesus, saying is it lawful to heal on the sabbath days?* (Matt. xii. 10, 11) *he said unto them, what man shall there be among you, that shall have one sheep, and if it fall into a pit on the sabbath day, will he not lay hold on it and lift it out? Wherefore it is lawful to do well on the sabbath days* (verse 12). It is lawful; that is, it is so far from being an infringement to the commandment, that the omission of an act of mercy

THE DUTY OF MERCY

even to an ox, or an ass, or a sheep that may stand in need of it would be a transgression against the benevolent design of it. For as he observes before in this chapter, *God will have mercy and not sacrifice* (verse 7), or he preferreth mercy to sacrifice; and he adds: *the Son of man is Lord even of the sabbath day* (verse 8); as much to say, every man is so far a lord of the sabbath, that though mercy and sacrifice are both required, yet when it so happens that the one cannot be performed but at the omission of the other, a man is justified as lord of the sabbath, and best fulfils the mind of the institutor to give mercy the preference. That by *son of man* he means mankind in general, is evident from the parallel place to this in the Gospel of St. Mark in which the last quoted sentence is introduced thus: *the sabbath was made for man, and not man for the sabbath* (ch. ii. 27). I.e. man was not created for the sake of keeping a sabbath; but the sabbath, after man was created, was instituted for the sake of *man*; and according to our Saviour's comment in the passages above mentioned, for the sake of *beast* likewise.

Remember the sabbath day is but another phrase for *remember mercy*; or, remember that the sabbath was ordained principally for the rest and refreshment of all concerned and mentioned in the commandment, whether child or servant or beast. That this was the principal design of the institution is further evident from the commandment of the lawgiver himself: *On the seventh day thou shalt rest: that thine ox and thine ass may rest* (here they are named first) *and the son of thy handmaid, and the stranger, may be refreshed* (Exod. xxiii. 12). And in the repetition of the law, it is thus written in fuller terms with a *memento* subjoined: *thou shalt not do any work, thou, nor thy son, nor thy daughter, nor thy man servant, nor thy maid servant, nor thine ox, nor thine ass, nor any of thy cattle, nor thy stranger that is within thy gates ... and remember that thou wast a servant in the land of Egypt* (Deut. v. 14); i.e. let the recollection of thy former hard servitude under the yoke of Egypt teach thee the duty and reasonableness of compassion and tenderness to all that labour on thy account, whether they be thy children, thy servants, thy cattle, the ox that ploughs for thee, the ass that carries thee or thy burden, or the stranger in thy gates.

By the *stranger that is within thy gates*, I suppose is meant, thy hireling, dayman, or journeyman, who is not of thy family, or so wholly dependent upon thee, as thy children, servants or cattle. Therefore the stranger is mentioned last, because, if you give him not rest, he can leave you when he pleases, and give rest to himself. But thy children, servants, and cattle, being always with thee, and under thy authority, and without redress, it is for their sakes the commandment seems principally intended; and therefore they are named before the stranger, to whom you ought to give such allowance for his six days' work, that he may be able to maintain himself on the sabbath day, without doing any manner of work; else you are instrumental to his breaking the sabbath.

It is said in the beginning of the commandment, *remember the sabbath day and keep it holy*:[1] and it is said in the conclusion of it, *the Lord blessed the sabbath day, and hallowed it.* God first gave a blessing to the labouring man and beast, by ordaining a sabbath, and then he hallowed or sanctified it to holy duties. In the divine mind mercy precedes sacrifice; for it is not said, *he hallowed it and blessed it,* but, *he blessed it, and hallowed it.* Again, it is said in the commandment,

[1] In the *Church Catechism*, the order is changed thus, *remember that thou keep holy the sabbath day,* which seems to intimate that holiness was the principal end of the institution. And again in the conclusion, instead of *The Lord blessed the sabbath day*, we read in the catechism, *the Lord blessed the seventh day.* Why the *order* of the words was changed in the beginning, or why the word *seventh* was substituted for the word *sabbath* in the conclusion, I enquire not; yet, in my humble opinion, the force and benevolent design of the commandment is much weakened by the transposition and mistranslation. For *sabbath* doth not imply *holiness*, though holiness is enjoined on the sabbath day. Nor doth *sabbath* denote *seventh*, though the seventh day is the sabbath day. H.P.

the Lord blessed the sabbath day, or the day of rest; for sabbath denotes rest; and the sabbath, if God had so pleased, might have been every *sixth* or *eighth* day, or without any special holiness. The commandment indeed hath appointed the sabbath or rest to be on the *seventh* day; and the rest of the seventh day affords leisure for spiritual duties; therefore God hath enjoined sanctification as well as rest on that day. But the first motive to the appointment was mercy to man and beast; for the *sabbath was made for man, and not man for the sabbath.* Therefore if thou, who art a master, workest on the sabbath day, you sin, because you do not sanctify it according to the commandment: but if you do no work thyself, and yet set your servants and cattle to work on that day, then you sin likewise, because you do not bless it according to the design of it. The commandment is twofold in its subject: *bless it,* and *sanctify* it; and it is twofold in its object: *do no work* and *require no work.* Consequently, the most scrupulous observance of the sabbath on thine own part, though you were to spend the whole day in acts of public and private devotion, and yet spare not the labour of thy servants and cattle, would not be *keeping the day unto the Lord;* it would be an imperfect and partial observance; it might be *sanctifying* it as to thyself, but it would not be *blessing* it, according to the institution of it, in mercy to the laborious man and beast; I say *man* and *beast,* for they are both expressly mentioned in the commandment; and the great creator, having considered them both, and having appointed a seventh day as a day of blessing, as well as of sanctification, will not accept thy *self-sanctification* of the day of sabbath, unless thine ox, and thine ass, and thy cattle, as well as thy children and servants, partake of the *blessing* of it.

I know indeed there may be cases of necessity, which require the labour of the cattle on the sabbath day, and I am not so precise as to suppose it a sin, in such cases, to make use of their labour; for as our saviour says, *the son of man is lord of the sabbath.*[1] But then it is my duty

---

[1] Matt. xii. 8.

to consider whether my beast hath in the preceding week fulfilled his six days task of labour. If he hath not fulfilled it, or has had some day or days of rest therein, I do not sin in the use of him. If he hath done his full task in the week, I ought to spare him for another beast that hath not fulfilled his task. But if necessity compels me to set the same beast to a seventh day of labour, who hath fulfilled his six days work, then I sin, if I do not remember, as soon as my urgent business is over, to assign him another day for his sabbath, in lieu of that which I have taken from him. For as sabbath was ordained for beast as well as man, though the beast is not capable of keeping the sabbath as a day of sanctification, he hath by the command of God a right to a sabbath as a day of rest and blessing.

And as God in his goodness hath appointed a sabbath or day of rest for the cattle, and hath thereby instructed us in the duty of mercy towards them, it necessarily follows that we ought not on *any* day of the week to overwork them, or lay too hard burdens upon them. For as the end of the commandment is charity, and founded upon mercy, every instance of unmercifulness is a transgression, though not of the letter, yet of the intent and extent of this commandment. Therefore if a man were to observe and keep the legal or established sabbath ever so scrupulously (neither doing any work himself, nor suffering any of his children, servants, or cattle to do any manner of work on *that* day), and yet on the *other* day of the week put them to work above their strength, or keep them too long to work without allowing them sufficient rest, I would not scruple to pronounce that man to be a daily sabbath breaker, because he daily transgresses that general law of mercy, to promote which a sabbath was principally instituted. Nor will the pretence that a working day is not the sabbath day justify an act of unmercifulness, any more than it will justify an act of unholiness; unless it can be shown that holiness and mercy, because particularly enjoined on the seventh day, are so limited to the seventh day, that for six days following a man has

THE DUTY OF MERCY

leave to be as profane and as cruel as he pleases. With God all days are alike, as to the essential duties of religion and morality. Holiness and mercy are the duties of every day; and he that said unto Israel, that even the sabbaths were an *abomination* unto him, and that when *they spread forth their hands* he would hide his face from them, and when they *made many prayers* he would not hear them, *because their hands were full of blood and cruelty* (Isa. i. 15), hath given us thereby to understand that he will as soon dispense with the devotion of the sabbath as with the mercy of it. Holiness and mercy are enjoined in one and the same commandment of sabbath, but with this difference according to the interpretation of Christ and Hosea (Matt. ix. 13. Hos. vi. 6) that God preferreth mercy to sacrifice. And as man and beast are both included in the same commandment of mercy, it follows that mercy to brutes is at all times no less a duty than mercy to men.

I have thus far endeavoured to prove that God careth for the cattle by the rules he has prescribed for our conduct towards them, in the articles of food and rest. But this is not all. For:

III. They have a further claim upon us of regard to their happiness, and tenderness in the usage of them. The goodness and providence of God respect not only the being, but the well-being of his creatures; not only their necessary wants, and what is absolutely their demand on the principles of strict justice, but also their ease and comfort, and what they have a reasonable and equitable claim to, on the principles of mercy and compassion.

A righteous man, saith Solomon, *regardeth the life of his beast: but the tender mercies of the wicked are cruel* (Prov. xii. 10). By *life* is sometimes to be understood desire,[1] or happiness; for what is life without happiness? Happiness is the salt of life, and in the proverb

---

[1] *Desire.* So is the *Hebrew* word NPSh translated in Eccles. vi. 9. H.P.

now before us is included in the word *life*, as appears from the antithesis – *that the tender mercies of the wicked are cruel*; or (as it is in the Hebrew and in the margin of our Bible) the bowels of the wicked are cruel. Now as *cruelty* and *wickedness* in the last sentence are put in opposition to *life* and *righteousness* in the former sentence, it is plain that by *life* must be meant kind and tender usage, as contrasted to hardheartedness and cruelty.

The above proverb is of general use to distinguish a righteous man from a wicked man. It is so plain that it hardly needs a comment; and it is so well known that it is frequently used and applied to the correction of cruelty by many persons, who consider not that, in the application of it, they accuse themselves of unrighteousness. For though it consists but of two parts in the *letter*, in *spirit* it describes three characters, viz. a *righteous* man, an *unrighteous* man, and a *wicked* man. As to the latter part of the proverb, the character is so discernible, that all further enquiries are needless. If I know that a man is cruel to his beast, I ask no more questions about him. He may be a noble man, or a rich man, or a polite man, or a sensible man, or a learned man, or an orthodox man, or a church man, or a puritan, or any thing else, it matters not; this I know, on the sacred word of a wise king, that, being *cruel* to his beast, he is a *wicked* man.

But, suppose a man is not cruel to his beast, and therefore not a wicked man; yet, according to the proverb, he may be an *unrighteous* man. And under this character I am afraid we may class thousands and ten thousands, who would on no account commit an act of cruelty. A righteous man is one that *regardeth*, and always keeps his eye on the rule of *right*; and whom no custom, or compliance, or fear of ridicule can ever pervert from his duty in matter of right. *The righteous showeth mercy*, saith David (Ps. xxxvii. 21); he doth not cloak it up in his breast, or smother it in helpless pity, but he *showeth* it; he attends to its calls, and brings it forth into action. Again (verse 26): *The righteous is ever merciful* (in the Hebrew, *all the day merciful*), full of mercy at all times, and on all occasions, and to every object of it, whether man or brute.

Every act of cruelty is wickedness. But, cruelty apart, the neglect of mercy is unrighteousness. A man may be very tender and full of pity, and yet be unmerciful, or not *show mercy*. If our beast suffers through our disregard or inattention to him, we cannot be said to be *ever* or *always* merciful, and we do not fulfil our duty towards him; for it is the part of a righteous man to show mercy as well as to profess it; and without this, our pretension of mercy is like the *unworking faith*, and the *unprofitable charity* described by St. James (ch. ii. 15, 16). We may sin by omission as well as commission; and though we be not *cruel* to him unto *wickedness*, we may be *regardless* of him unto *unrighteousness*.

The three characters, therefore, described in the above proverb are these: the man who so hardeneth his bowels to the yearnings of compassion that, without the least emotion of pity, he can commit an act of *cruelty* to his beast, is a wicked man; the man who *regardeth* the happiness of his beast, who *showeth mercy* to it, by attending to all its wants and infirmities, and who endeavours to make it as easy and as happy as its nature and condition will admit, is a *righteous* man; but the man who regardeth it *not,* who is careless and indifferent about it, though he may not be hardhearted and cruel to it, yet inasmuch as he regardeth it not, he is an unrighteous man; for *the righteous man regardeth* the life, the desire, and the happiness *of his beast*.

If any (saith St. Paul in the epistle to Timothy before mentioned, and in the same chapter in which he quotes from the law of Moses, *thou shalt not muzzle the ox that treadeth out the corn) provide not for his own, and especially for those of his own house, he hath denied the faith, and is worse than an infidel*. This sentence deserves the particular notice of masters and families. All that are committed to the care and management of the head of the house, whether children, servants, cattle, or hireling are parts of the family, as I showed before in my observation on the fourth commandment. They are all, therefore, *of his own house*; and being such, it is the duty of the head of the house to *provide* – that is, to have *providence* over, to take care of, and attend to – every member of the family within doors and without doors. It is no excuse in the master if a beast suffers through the *cruelty*, or through the *neglect* of his servant. For if the beast could speak, he would make his complaint to the master, as the proper person to take cognizance of the injury; but as he cannot speak for himself, it is the master's duty to speak for him; and, unless he is worse than an infidel, he will speak for him without being spoken to. But if he thinks any one in his service beneath his notice, he is unworthy of the service of that one. And if he never enquires or concerns himself about any of those that are committed to his care, or is negligent as to any of them, he cannot be said to *provide for those of his own house;* he is negligent as to the great duty of mercy on which the gospel is founded; he therefore denieth the faith, and is pronounced by the apostle to be worse than an infidel.

But the righteous man regardeth the happiness even of his beast, and provideth for him, as for one *of his own*, and *of his own house*. It is not enough that his beast looks well, he enquires whether it fares well; for many times the most cruel means are used (by vain and foolish servants to please their as vain and foolish masters) to make the beast appear sleek, shining, and of graceful carriage without, whilst the poor creature is rotten and suffers unutterable misery within. As he is righteous, he is merciful; and being merciful upon a righteous principle, he is ever merciful, and showeth mercy to him in every respect. He muzzleth not the beast *that treadeth out his corn*, or that labours for his profit or his pleasure: he taketh care that he is ungirded; he giveth him straw and provender; he *leadeth him forth to the watering*; he alloweth him the *blessing of sabbath*; and to protect him from the inclemency of the weather, he followeth the example of the patriarch Jacob, who when *he built himself an house, made booths for his cattle* (Gen. xxxiii. 17). He attends to all his wants and infirmities and considers well his age, his stature, and his strength. If young, he breaketh not the back of his tender colt, but waiteth till his sinews are strengthened unto perfection. He neither nicks him nor docks him, but takes him such as God made him. If aged, he galleth not his feeble sides, nor addeth one weight extraordinary to the weight of his years; but, with a sense of gratitude, he rewardeth his path and faithful services with renewed attention, forbearance, and indulgence. He saith within himself: "this beast by toil and sweat hath administered to my pleasure or to my profit for many years past; and now that he is no longer able to perform my work, shall I dismiss him as a creature not worthy of my future protection? Shall I subject him to the caprice, or abuse, or inexperienced servitude of a new, and, it may be, of a cruel and mercenary master? If he is not fit for *my* work, he is not fit for *any* work. And shall I curse the age of my beast because he hath worn himself out in my service? Or the gain, which I have acquired by his labour, shall I corrode it by the price of his blood? *No.* If I chop not his hay; if I grind not his corn; if I assist not the decay and unevenness of his teeth by conducting him to the longest, mildest, and tenderest grass in my pasture; I will yet testify my approbation of his former service, by putting an instant period to all his pain."

Whether young or old, whether strong or weak, whether sound or maimed, the righteous man proportions the work to the ability of the brute, and balances them both in the just scale of equity. As he *regardeth* the happiness of his beast, so he *provideth* for the ease of it. And however this may appear a circumstance of very small moment, yet, to guard us against greater instances of injustice, and to show how extremely cautious we should be in offending against the brutes, who are entirely in our power, and have no means of redress, we find to this purpose the following precept in the sacred law of Moses:

Thou shalt not plough with an ox and an ass together

(Deut. xxii. 10). Some have thought that St. Paul alludes to this precept in 2 Cor. vi. 14.[1] If the apostle had it in view, it is a mere allusion to it, and not an interpretation of it. It may confirm it, but does not supersede it. And even if we were to admit that St. Paul's supposed allusion to it was intended as the true and proper interpretation and sign of the precept, still it exhibits to us the wisdom and benevolence of the lawgiver, in delivering a civil law in words which should, at the same time, convey the idea of mercy to brutes. But Aben Ezra, a Spanish Jew commentator, by making this observation on the passage before us, *viz.* that *the strength of an ass is not as the strength of an ox*, intimates that he and his nation understood it in the literal sense, and that it was intended as a general rule of mercy, to adapt the work and the burden to the strength of the labourer.[2] The prohibition therefore, *Thou shalt not plough with an ox and an ass together*, implies thus much at least, that we shall not set a weak beast to keep pace with, nor to do the work of a strong beast; nor put him to any work which he is incapable of performing. Such usage is disregard, neglect, or non-attention to their strength and ability. It is both foolish and unjust; and, in the strictest sense, it is an abuse of them. And if the abuse of the cattle by putting them to improper work, or subjugating them to unequal yokes, is a transgression against the divine law, and every transgression is sin; to add cruelty to abuse, or to ill treat, and torment them with barbarity and unbridled fury, must be a sin of a heinous nature indeed. And of this we have an instance and proof in the case of Balaam, who was sent for by Balak, king of Moab, to curse the people of Israel (Num. xxii).

As Balaam was riding upon his ass (the usual manner

[1] *Be ye not unequally yoked together with unbelievers.*
[2] To the same purpose saith the learned and ingenious Cardinal Cajetan: Hoc præceptum metaphorice intelligendum est, ut dispares vires hominum non æque graventur, nec exigantur æqua ab imparibus: optime enim sub hae metaphora præceptum hoc morale memoriæ commendatur. Cajeten, *in Loco.* H.P.

of travelling in his country), and two servants with him, the ass saw an apparition which the rider did not see; and the timorous beast turned aside out of the path into a field; upon which Balaam in a passion smote the ass, and turned her into the road again. As he proceeded further, they came to a road between two walls. The ass saw the apparition again, and, starting aside, crushed her master's foot against one of the walls; and Balaam smote the ass a second time. At last they came to a very narrow place, where there was no way to turn, either to the right hand, or to the left: and the ass, seeing the apparition the third time, was so exceedingly terrified, that all her strength forsook her, and she fell down to the ground under Balaam. Her master, instead of reflecting with himself that there must be something extraordinary in this case (as the ass was not wont to start or to stumble), and instead of asking the two servants that were with him, if they saw any thing uncommon, or could account for the shyness of the beast, was so overcome with passion and rage, that he unmercifully beats the poor creature with a staff. The fallen beast, sensible of her own pain and of her master's cruelty and injustice, had she been endued with speech and reason, would probably have expostulated with him on her hard treatment the first and the second time. But alas! She was dumb, and could not open her mouth. But now, at the third time, when Balaam's anger was kindled into a flame, and ascended to its height, the Lord himself was pleased to interpose in behalf of the abused animal by opening the mouth of the ass; *and she said unto Balaam, what have I done unto thee, that thou has smitten me three times?* Behold a miracle! The dumb ass speaks. Behold a greater miracle, the rider was not struck dumb with amazement at the voice of the beast! Infatuated even unto madness, he considers not the overruling power of God herein, but being as blind as he was cruel, he replies to the complaint of the ass: *Because thou hast mocked me; I would there were a sword in my hand, for now would I kill thee.* Cruelty is the last step to murder. He first beat the ass cruelly, and then because she complained and reproved him, he would have killed her. But the Lord, observing the malicious rage of the man, blinded with fury, and hardened in his wickedness, instead of being reformed by the miracle, was pleased at length, as he had before opened the mouth of the ass, now to open the eyes of Balaam, who sees an *angel of the Lord standing in the way.* He had wished for a sword in his own hand to kill the ass, and now he beholds the angel of the Lord with a drawn sword in *his* hand ready to kill him. He called for a sword, and a sword immediately appears. And the man, who had cruelly treated his beast for starting and stumbling to avoid the sword of the avenger, now *boweth his own head, and falls flat on his face.* The case of the man and the brute is now the same in point of fear: the appearance of the angel was no less terrifying to the master than to the beast that carried him; and justly might the angel have requited Balaam in kind for his cruelty. But as God is more merciful to sinful men, than men are to unsinning brutes, the angel of the Lord was pleased to sheath his sword: and though he came to Balaam with a message from the Lord of very great importance, yet he postpones the delivery of his errand till he had first reproved and convinced Balaam of his wickedness and cruelty in smiting the ass, which was a sin deserving notice and reproof. And that the reproof might be more striking to Balaam, the angel makes use of the very words which the ass had spoken before: *What have I done to thee,* said the ass, *that thou hast smitten me these three times?* And the angel said unto Balaam, *wherefore hast thou smitten thine ass these three times?* To the question of the ass, Balaam had replied, *because thou hast mocked me, and I would there were a sword in my hand, for now would I kill thee.* But when the angel asked him the very same question, his tone was changed; and we hear not a word about *mocking,* or *wishing for a sword to kill her;* but a confession of sin, and an apology of ignorance. His stout and stubborn heart trembled; the consciousness of his guilt, and the sense of his folly and

THE DUTY OF MERCY

injustice in smiting the innocent beast, touched him to the quick; and, in spite of his pride, passion, and cruelty, extorted from him this frank confession: *I have sinned* (verse 34): *and Balaam said unto the angel of the Lord, I have sinned.*

But perhaps it will be objected that this confession, *I have sinned*, alludes to his going on the wicked design to curse the Israelites, unless restrained by the overruling power of God. I grant that cursing and cruelty are kindred sins. Experience tells us they frequently go together. And I acknowledge that the first intent of Balaam to undertake this journey was wicked and sinful, though he had a permission to go; and he might well say on that account, *I have sinned*. But it does not appear to me that he had that in view when he made his confession. His sin consisted in *smiting* the ass; for the confession is the response to the angel's question. The angel did not say, *Why dost thou proceed in thy cursed design?* But, *Why hast thou smitten thine ass these three times?* It was to this question that Balaam replied, *I have sinned.* And though the angel told him that it was he that stood in the way, and occasioned the ass to turn aside, yet Balaam does not look upon his own ignorance of this circumstance as a justification of his cruelty. It might alleviate his guilt in some measure, but did not clear it. And though he apologizes for his conduct by saying, *I knew not that thou stoodest in the way* (which shows that the sin referred to was smiting the ass), yet the *action* itself being cruel, and the effect of passion, he introduces his apology with the confession of guilt; and it amounts to this – *though I knew not that thou stoodest in the way against me, yet I have sinned, in smiting the ass.*

I wish this part of the sacred history were more duly and gravely attended to than I fear it is. It has been treated with contempt and ridicule; as absurd in itself, and unworthy a place in holy writ. But, for my own part, I can see nothing absurd or ridiculous in supposing that the great Creator, with whom all things are possible, and who thought it not beneath him to create the various orders of animals from the highest to the lowest, should care for the meanest of them. We men, indeed, to show how unworthy we are of our own dignity, are apt to despise and insult the inferior animals, as below our notice or regard, nay, as objects of our contempt and maliciousness. But the great God *seeth not as man seeth*; with him nothing is contemptible. He *saw every thing that he had made, and behold it was very good.*[1] And as God is love,[2] the extent of his love is the perfection of his goodness. Where is the absurdity then, that a messenger from heaven, who was sent for reproof or direction to an obstinate and passionate man, observing him to offend against the law of mercy, should check and reprove him for his cruelty? The angel's silence as to this particular would, indeed, have been a matter of wonder; and we should from thence have inferred that cruelty to brutes is no sin because an angel of mercy took no notice of it in Balaam. But as the angel's errand was a message of love and mercy unto Israel in the first design of it, it was highly consistent with the character of a messenger of love and mercy to keep them in view in his whole transaction, of which his gentle expostulation to Balaam, as well as his forbearance in sparing him, are illustrious proofs. I do not say that the angel was sent on purpose to rebuke Balaam for this sin; it is plain he was not: for the angel was present, and the ass saw him, before her master smote her the first time; but it displeased the angel so much that he withdrew himself for a season. He would have appeared the second time, but the same cause produced the same effect. But now at the third time, the just indignation of the heavenly messenger was kindled at the foolish passion and cruelty of Balaam. He could no longer contain, and yet, as if he deemed the man unworthy to hear *his* voice, he opens the mouth of the injured ass that she might plead her own cause with *human* voice; and by the strange-

---

[1] Gen. i. 31.
[2] 1 John iv. 8, 16.

THE DUTY OF MERCY

ness of the miracle convince her master of his folly and injustice.[1] But when the miracle had no effect upon the infatuated man, then did the angel exhibit himself in the posture of vengeance, and waves his important message till he had first corrected Balaam for this cruelty. And as this history was to be handed down to us in record, he would not let slip this opportunity of teaching mankind by divine interposition the duty of mercy, and the sin of cruelty to brute animals. And the more miraculous this history is, it is the more striking, and deserving our notice and remembrance.

If it should be said it is impossible an ass could speak,[2] I answer in few words: it is blasphemy to determine the power of the great God of nature. But whether the ass *really* spoke; or whether it was the voice of the angel thrown so as to seem to Balaam to proceed from the mouth of the ass; or whether it was a *created* voice; or an *impression* upon the ear of Balaam; still it was a divine interposition, not unbecoming an angel, in favour of suffering innocence. Or even if we were to admit that there was neither speech nor hearing on any part, but that it was only a vision, or a fancy of the imagination; or, that the whole narration is but a *parable*; still, it has its use, and answers the purpose of the sacred writer to represent to us the sin and injustice of cruelty. But I desire it may be observed that this narration has the sanction of an important truth stamped upon it by St. Peter in his second epistle, in which he tells us that Balaam was *rebuked for his iniquity*, and that *the dumb ass, speaking with man's voice, forbad the madness of the prophet* (2 Pet. ii. 16).

It seems, then, that this ridiculed piece of sacred history has the authority of both the Old and New Testament for its support. And it deserves the more to

---

[1] *It pleased God to open the mouth of the ass in a complaint of the injustice of her master, to beat her for not going forward.* Josephus, *Jewish Antiquities*, Book iv. ch. 5.

[2] See an ingenious vindication of this piece of scripture history, in the learned Bishop Newton's *Dissertations on the Prophecies*, Vol. 1. H.P.

be noticed by us, and I have dwelt the longer upon it, because this particular instance of passion and cruelty is, I believe, more common than any other; and that too in men otherwise compassionate enough. For, say, did *you* never whip, or spur, or ill treat your horse, when at any time he has startled or stumbled? Was your passion never excited thereby? And did you not almost wish there had been a sword in your hand to kill him? Pardon me, reader, for putting the question home to you. I hope you can answer in the negative; but it is an instance common every day. If you are innocent as to this point, well for thee; and I turn myself to another that will plead guilty. And to the former question, I ask him further: did you, when your passion was over, lay your hand upon your beast, and say in the words of Balaam, I have sinned? I fear not. Then give me leave to tell you: you have so many sins still unrepented of; you have erred with Balaam, but not repented with him; and the sword of the angel is still drawn against thee. But repent in time, that he may sheath it. And whenever it so happens for the future, that your horse either stumbles or starts, I intreat thee to call this to mind. Know that your beast is not to blame. He no more loves to be affrighted than you do. It is no more agreeable to him to make a false step than it is to yourself. He feels the pain of the jarr as well as you. Therefore smite him not. But remember this history, and add not sin unto sin. The angel of the Lord is with you, though you see him not; and, in this case, sometimes withstands thee. Say not, my horse stumbles, and therefore I smite him; but consider that, whilst you ride, your horse goes a-foot; and a fixed stone or hillock, a sharp flint, or a pinched and uneasy shoe, might cause even yourself to stumble, if you were to travel on foot; and you would think it hard to be chastised for an involuntary or forced trip. Do not then unto others as you would be unwilling should be done to you. Say not, my horse starts, and therefore I smite him; and I correct him, because he is timorous; but consider that you have your passions, as well as your horse. Else, why the blood in thy face? Or, why the paleness of countenance on these occasions? The passion of anger, or the passion of fear, do then predominate in thyself. Learn first to subdue the sudden emotions of thine own passions, and then endeavour to correct his fears. I will grant, if you please, that his passion of *fear* may be foolish; but so is your passion of *anger*; and your folly is greater than his, if what you sometimes say is true: that a man has more reason than a horse. You have reason, and use it not; your horse has no reason, therefore he cannot use it. Your horse has not reason to conquer his fears, whilst you have both reason and power to subdue your own passion. Your horse offends and cannot help it; you offend, and may help it. I leave it to your own judgement to determine whether you or your horse deserves most to be corrected. In short, to smite your horse because he stumbles or starts, is irrationality and weakness. And if you will not allow your boasted reason to correct the fear of your horse by gentleness, forbearance, or skilful management, but think to overcome his fears by whip, spur, and barbarity, you expose yourself to the just and severe correction of the angel, who *withstands thee, because thy way is perverse before him.*[1] And instances are not uncommon, when his just anger is so provoked at the cruelty of man in this case, that though he doth not open the mouth of the beast to reprove his rider (as he once did, and which there is no occasion to do a second time), yet he appoints the injured beast to plead his own cause another way, in being the instrument of punishment, and sometimes the executioner of death, without allowing a moment's leisure to make the short confession of Balaam: *I have sinned.* The inference is obvious, that to lose life by the prancing or unruliness of a horse, excited thereto by barbarity, because he may have started or stumbled, is to die in an act of sin.

We are told by the prophet Micah that when Balaam, who had sinned in thus passionately smiting the ass,

[1] Num. xxii. 32.

was afterwards consulted by Balak the king of Moab (at whose request he had undertaken this journey) how he *might know the righteousness of the Lord* (that is, how he might recommend himself to, and best please, Jehovah the god of Israel, whose power he was now sensible of, and whose favour he desired to obtain), Balaam gives this instruction unto the king: *he hath showed thee, O man, what is good; and what doth the Lord require of thee, but to do justly, and to love mercy, and to walk humbly with thy God* (Micah vi. 8).

In this advice to the king, Balaam seems to allude to the three great duties of justice, mercy and humility, against which he himself had so notoriously transgressed in smiting his ass three times. To strike the beast that *never before since she was his unto that day was wont to stumble or start*,[1] because now she started for the first time, was injustice. To strike her a second time, and a third time to beat her with a staff, and to wish for a sword in his hand to kill her, was cruelty. And to suppose, because the ass was his own, that he had an absolute and unaccountable power over her to use her as unjustly and as cruelly as he pleased, was taking too much upon human nature; it was contemptuously ill treating one of God's creatures, a useful and an innocent creature, and a beast whose simplicity and natural stupidity (peculiar to the ass, that it may go through its drudgery with less reluctance), should have recommended her to her master's mercy and forbearance; it was over-valuing himself; it was under-rating his beast; and, in short, it was pride. Balaam, therefore, neither did justly, nor loved mercy, nor walked humbly. But no sooner was he brought to a sense of his crime, than he confessed: *I have sinned*; and as if that were not enough, at the hazard and expense of all his hopes of preferment, he, moreover, preaches in the court of Moab the great duties of justice, mercy and humility. Hast thou sinned then with Balaam? With him confess that *thou hast sinned*. Perfect thy confession, and fulfil

[1] Num. xxii. 30.

thy repentance, by taking every opportunity assiduously to inculcate into others these great and necessary duties. You will thereby give a more sure proof of thy repentance, and better please the Lord, than with thousands of rams, or ten thousands of rivers of oil: for, *the Lord desireth mercy and not sacrifice, and the knowledge of God more than burnt offerings.*[1] If thou wert *to give thy first born for thy transgression, or the fruit of thy body for the sin of thy soul,*[2] it would avail thee nothing; it would be worse than nothing; it would be adding one sin to another. But *the Lord hath showed thee, O man, what is good,* what in this case thou ought to do, and what he will accept and require of thee: viz. *to do justly, and to love mercy, and to walk humbly with thy God.*

Are justice, mercy and humility, the criteria of righteousness? Then injustice, unmercifulness, and pride, which frequently go together, and point to each other, and are all comprehended in the idea of cruelty to brutes, must be sure tokens of sin and wickedness. And in particular, is the Love of mercy a mean whereby to know the righteousness of the Lord? Is it a duty which the Lord will require of thee, and according to which thou wilt be accepted? Then, as you would avoid the imputation of unrighteousness, and as you desire to secure the favour of thy God, let mercy be shown in the treatment of thy beast. But it is not the counsel of Balaam only; it is likewise, as was before observed, the judgment of the wise king of Israel, that mercy and cruelty are the signs whereby to distinguish a righteous man, and a wicked man: *A righteous man regardeth the life or happiness of his beast: but the tender mercies or bowels of the wicked are cruel* (Prov. xii. 10). If a man is cruel to his beast, he must be a wicked man. If he is not cruel to him, yet if he regardeth him not, he is not a righteous man; that is, he is an unrighteous man. And as unrighteousness is a footstep to cruelty, well might

[1] Hosea vi. 6.
[2] Micah vi. 7.

David class *wickedness, unrighteousness,* and *cruelty* together in one and the same deprecation: *Deliver me, O my God, out of the hand of the wicked, out of the hand of the unrighteous and cruel man* (Ps. lxxi. 4).

I have hitherto confined myself to those particular passages in scripture which contain and enjoin the duties towards the cattle, that are more especially under our own care, in the articles of food, rest, forbearance and tender usage; because in some of these instances we are very apt to offend. And here we cannot but admire the wisdom and goodness of God, who, in his mercy to the brutes, has given us rules for our conduct towards them, in all these instances; and has been graciously pleased to transcribe them from the Old into the New Testament, to teach us that mercy to the cattle is a virtue as indispensably requisite under the gospel of Christ, as under the law of Moses. Examine yourself then by these rules and precepts of mercy, and apply these cases to your own conduct, and you will plainly perceive that when you withhold from your beast his due quantity and proportion of meat or drink, you muzzle the ox that treadeth out your corn. When you overwork him, or give him not his proper rest, you do not *remember the sabbath to keep it,* according to the intent of the commandment. When you abuse, or unequally yoke him, or put him to a work which he is incapable of performing, you may be said to *plough with an ox and an ass together. When you regard him not, you are an unrighteous man.* When you are cruel to him, you are a wicked man. When you beat him for stumbling or starting, or suffer your passion of anger to be excited by his untowardness or stupidity, you partake in the sin of Balaam, and *your way is perverse before God.* In all, or any of these or any other instances of cruelty, you forfeit the name of a righteous man, whose distinguishing character is this, that he regardeth the life and happiness of his beast; you *know not the righteousness of the Lord;* you consider not what is good, nor what it is that he requireth of thee; and, in short, you neither do justly, nor love mercy, nor walk

THE DUTY OF MERCY

humbly before thy God.

Thus far we have considered the duties, particularly enjoined in holy scripture with regard to our *own* cattle. But let it not be inferred from hence, that mercy is a *limited* virtue; cases may and often do occur, in which the exercise of it is to be practised and extended beyond our own province. To neglect or abuse, or ill treat our own cattle, is cruelty of a heinous nature; because they have a *right* to our care and tenderness: and *if any man provide not for his own, and especially for those of his own house, he hath denied the faith, and is worse than an infidel.* But our mercy and regard is not to rest there. It is further our duty to be always ready to relieve and succour the miserable, whether known or unknown to us. Any beast in distress, be it ox, or ass, or sheep, or other animal, has a claim upon us of assistance. For in the law of Moses we find it thus written:

Thou shalt not see thy brother's ox or his sheep go astray, and hide thyself from them: thou shalt in any case bring them again unto thy brother. And if thy brother be not nigh unto thee, or if thou know him not (i.e. if it is the beast of a stranger), *then thou shalt bring it unto thine own house, and it shall be with thee until thy brother seek after it, and thou shalt restore it to him again.*[1] (Deut. xxii. 1, 2). The scope of this precept doth not consist merely in the rule of justice to restore the lost beast to thy brother or neighbour but in the rule of mercy and compassion to the beast itself; else it might have been enough to drive it to a pond, or tie it to a gate, till the owner should come to enquire after it. But the law saith: *Thou shalt bring it into thine own house, and it shall be with thee.* As the finder, thou art the temporary possessor of it in trust for the right owner; and thou shalt take as much care of the lost beast, as if it were thine own, till the owner recovers it again.

And as the law has thus *provided* for the beast that is going astray, so no less indulgent is it to the beast that

---

[1] *The owner paying the charges of keeping it from the time it was brought to the house, till its being restored.* St. Patrick.

hath met with an accident. For in the fourth verse of this chapter, we have another commandment of mercy respecting the cattle that are not our own property: *Thou shalt not see thy brother's ass or his ox fall down by the way, and hide thyself from them: thou shalt surely help him to lift them up again.* This law seems expressly enjoined for the sake of the beast; for it can hardly be supposed that if you were to see thy brother, or thy neighbour, in any kind of difficulty or distress, you would forbear to help him. Brotherhood and neighbourhood have this demand upon thee without a law. It is not said, therefore, *Thou shalt not hide thyself from him*; but, thou shalt not hide thyself from *them*; that is, from the ass or the ox that are fallen down. Thou shalt not hide thyself, or draw back, as if ashamed or unwilling to do an act of charity to distressed because brutal innocence; but thou shalt surely, or at the peril of a breach of a divine commandment, help him to lift them up again, and afford all the succour to them that thou art able to give.

But what if the brute that is going astray, or fallen down, is not my brother's, nor my neighbour's? What if I know it to belong to a man, who hath done me repeated injuries; an open enemy; a man that hateth me; who rejoiceth at my adversity; and who, if he was to see my beast going astray or fallen down, would let him go, or keep him down rather than help him? Am I to provide for, or to regard the beast of such an enemy, and of the man that hateth me? To this I might reply in the words of the meek and merciful Jesus, *Love thine enemy, and do good to him that hateth thee.*[1] But as the question supposeth that thou hast not yet attained unto this high degree of Christian perfection, let us return back to the law, which is *a schoolmaster to bring us unto Christ,*[2] and let us enquire what that says as to this point. But I shall first beg leave to ask thee a question or two. Is the beast of thine enemy an enemy

[1] Luke vi. 27.
[2] Gal. iii. 24.

THE DUTY OF MERCY

unto thee? Doth the beast hate thee? Did the beast ever willingly and designedly do thee an injury? Doth the beast retain any grudge against thee? Did the dumb beast ever slander or belie thee? Or, did the irrational beast every contrive any plot or device against thee? I believe thou wilt answer, no. Then, what is it to thee, with regard to the brute, that his master is thine enemy? A creature endued with a sense of feeling, who never did thee an injury, is in distress or pain; you have it in your power to help him; but he happeneth to be the property of a man that hateth thee; therefore this distressed but innocent brute must continue to suffer pain because, without any choice of his own, he belongs to thine enemy. Is this good reasoning? Or, is it at all consistent with the rule of justice or equity, that the innocent should suffer for the guilty? Or that the master's enmity to thee should cancel the duty of compassion and relief to the distressed and unoffending brute? I think not. But as this is only *human* reasoning, let us refer for direction to the positive and written law of God. And blessed be his goodness and mercy, that he hath been pleased to give us therein a commandment full and clear as to both these points; whether we see our enemy's beast going astray, or fallen down under his burden.

I. *If thou meet thine enemy's ox or his ass going astray, thou shalt surely bring it back to him again* (Exod. xxiii. 4). We may observe above in the case of a beast going *astray*, if it be the beast of thy brother, or neighbour, you are required to send it *to him again*; but if it be the beast of a stranger, then to take it to your *own house*, and to keep it, till you hear of the owner, and he sends for it. But in the present case the owner is thine enemy; as such, you know him, and most likely where he lives; you are not required therefore to take this lost beast to your own house, and keep it till the owner comes to enquire after it; for as the owner is your enemy, you, or your servants, might be tempted, on that account, to neglect or misuse it; but you are to send it back to your enemy, or at least to give him immediate notice that you have found it: *If thou meet thine enemy's ox or his ass going astray, thou shalt surely bring it back to him again.* And this you may do, without having any intercourse with thine enemy. You may send the beast home to him without seeing the man. You may do an act of kindness to the brute, and yet avoid the disagreeable circumstance of a parley. But:

II. Suppose you should see the beast *fallen down under his burden,* and the master with him. The man is thine enemy and hateth thee; and we will suppose too that you do not much love him; at least, that you have said you will have no connection at all with him; you will not even be seen in his company; much less will you undertake any work for him, or co-operate with him in any respect. Yet what saith the law to this? *If thou see the ass of him that hateth thee, lying under his burden, and wouldst forbear to help him, thou shalt surely help with him* (Exod. xxiii. 5). The law maketh not the least allowance in the duty of mercy to an innocent brute. The beast is in a state of painful suffering; he is fallen down, and requires instant relief. All animosity apart, and no dispensation granted, thou art commanded to lend a helping hand to the man that hateth thee, how disagreeable soever the task may be; and though you would forbear to help the man himself out of difficulty, because he is thine enemy and hateth thee, yet, for the sake of the poor creature, *thou shalt surely help with him* to lift him up. The ass is not to bear his master's transgression. The beast is innocent, though the master is guilty; and to refuse to the wretched brute thy attention and assistance, because the master hateth thee, is a weak, a cruel and a misplaced revenge.

If any brute then be in distress, and we know it, and are able to relieve him, it is our duty, and we are commanded to do it, whether the owner be known or unknown to us; and whether he be our friend or our foe. And if we are required to show mercy to the cattle of strangers and enemies, it is self-evident that we ought to abound in mercy to our own cattle, whether oxen, or asses, or horses, or any other kind. Horses, indeed, are

THE DUTY OF MERCY

not mentioned in any of the foregoing precepts and examples, because they were not in common use amongst the Jews, who ploughed with oxen, and rode and carried burdens upon asses; yet the rule of equity extends the commandment to *all* the creatures entrusted to our care, and included under the general denomination of cattle, which we are neither to muzzle, nor to overwork, nor to overload, nor to ill treat, nor in any wise to neglect or abuse.

I cannot entirely quit this subject concerning the creatures which are appointed for our service, without taking notice of one remarkable instance of the compassion of God towards them, recorded in the sacred writings. Our dominion over the cattle is apt to suggest to us the notion that, as they are so much inferior to men, and made as it were dependent upon us for their daily bread, they are removed at too great a distance to be objects of the divine love. Yet there was a day when these very brutes were the mediators between the vengeance of an offended God, and the provocations of sinful men; when they stood in the gap, between the sentence of judgment denounced, and the execution of it. For, when the hand of the Almighty was lifted up to destroy the great city of Nineveh for the wickedness of them that dwelt therein, the innocence of the cattle, as well as the innocence of the little children, averted, for a time, the wrath of indignant heaven. *Shall I not spare Nineveh,* saith the Lord unto Jonah, *should I not spare Nineveh, that great city, wherein are more than six score thousand persons that cannot discern between their right hand and their left hand; and also much cattle* (Jonah iv. 11).

Extensive no less than compassionate is the sublime and benevolent precept of our blessed Saviour: *be ye merciful, as your father is also merciful* (Luke vi. 36). With what views, or into what narrow compass, the pride or selfishness of men may have contracted this heavenly precept, I ask not; but the inference I would draw from it is this: that if God hath displayed his goodness and mercy towards the brutes in his creation of them, in his providence over them, and in his gracious interposition on their behalf in prescribing rules in his written word for our conduct towards them, then it becomes an indispensable duty on the part of men, in conformity to the divine goodness, to be merciful to them likewise; else we limit the extent of this divine and important commandment, and are not *merciful as our Father is merciful*. But let it be further noted, that the heavenly pattern and precept of mercy is moreover strengthened and secured with the blessing and promise of mercy. *Blessed are the merciful*, saith Jesus, the son of the blessed, *for they shall obtain mercy* (Matt. v. 7). And similar hereunto was the exhortation of Jesus the son of Sirach: *Make way for every work of mercy; for every man shall find according to his works* (Ecclus. xvi. 14). The obvious meaning of both these sentences is the same: be thou merciful, and God will be merciful unto thee; be thou cruel, and God will requite thy cruelty according to its work.

To be *merciful as our father is merciful*, and to *make way for every work of mercy*, necessarily imply that it is our duty to extend or show mercy to *every* object of it. No creature is so insignificant, but whilst it has life, it has a right to happiness. To deprive it of happiness is injustice; and to put it to unnecessary pain is cruelty. It is very unreasonable, therefore, if not foolish in men, to estimate the *degree* of the sin of cruelty to any creature by the value we set upon the creature itself; or to suppose that the difference of size, or difference of beauty, are foundations of real difference as to the *feelings* of brutes. A fly has feeling as well as an ox; and a toad has as much right to happiness as a canary bird; for the same God made the ox, and the fly, and the toad and the bird. It is true, we have an aversion to some creatures, and we are better affected towards some than to others; but we ought not to put any of them to pain, if we can avoid it; for cruelty to a brute is odious and abominable, whether it be to a beast, or a bird, or a fish or a worm. Be the creature never so insignificant in our estimation, we cannot put it to any degree of pain

THE DUTY OF MERCY

without violation of the laws of nature; because every living creature is the work of the God of nature.

According to the divine law, mercy is a duty of that universal extent, that it will not be dispensed with even in the accidental, and yet not uncommon circumstance, of finding a bird's nest. *If a bird's nest chance to be before thee in the way in any tree, or on the ground, whether they be young ones, or eggs, and the dam sitting upon the young, or upon the eggs, thou shalt not take the dam with the young: but thou shalt in any wise let the dam go ... that it may be well with thee, and that thou mayest prolong thy days* (Deut. xxii. 6). Were there no other text throughout the Bible from which to prove the duty of mercy to brute animals but this only, this alone is enough to rest it upon. The goodness and condescension of the great creator in this seemingly trifling instance of a bird's nest is so remarkably displayed; and our attention to the law, and our compassion to the distressed bird, is enforced with the promise of a blessing of so extraordinary a kind, for so small a service; that to reflect upon it at all, one would think it sufficient to mollify the hardest heart, and to confound the pride of the greatest man upon Earth. Indeed it is a precept so striking, so important, and so abundant in love, that I cannot avoid repeating it over again: *If a bird's nest chance to be before thee in the way, in any tree, or on the ground, whether they be young ones or eggs, and the dam is sitting upon the young, or upon the eggs, thou shalt not take the dam with the young: but thou shalt in any wise let the dam go ... that it may be well with thee, and that thou mayest prolong thy days.*

I am sorry there should be any occasion (though, when I consider the remissness of many parents in not instructing their children in the duty of mercy to birds, I find myself necessitated) to remind them that the blessing annexed in this commandment to this instance of compassion to the bird, is the *very same* as the blessing subjoined to the fifth commandment of the decalogue, in which parents are so deeply interested.

Honour thy father and thy mother, saith the law of Sinai, *that thy days may be long upon the land* (Exod. xx. 12); or, as it is more fully expressed in the repetition of the law, *that thy days may be prolonged, and that it may go well with thee* (Deut. v. 16). The words are similar to the words in the precept before us: *thou shalt in any wise let the dam go, that it may be well with thee, and that thou mayest prolong thy days.* Length of days, attainable by all men, is in the right hand of wisdom. Riches and honour, which can be the portion of but a few, are only the ornaments *of her left hand.*[1] But it is her right hand gift, the most noble and venerable gift which wisdom can bestow, that is promised as the reward of reverence of parents, and yet not deemed misplaced nor thrown away upon the *merciful and compassionate.*

Thou shalt not take the dam with the young, says the precept, *but thou shalt in any wise let the dam go.* This may mean that thou shalt take neither dam nor young, unless you find the nest upon the ground, in which case the young ones may be bruised or hurt by the fall, or trodden under foot; and then it is a kindness to take them away and dispatch them. But whether you take the young or not, *thou shalt in any wise let the dam go.* Thou shalt not add one affliction to another. The tender mother is bereaved of her children, and is not this sorrow sufficient? But wilt thou cruelly deprive her of her liberty likewise, and of the pleasure or possibility of having other young in their stead? No. *Thou shalt not take the dam with the young; but thou shalt in any wise let the dam go, that it may be well with thee, and that thou mayest prolong thy days.* Oh, that all parents would duly and seriously reflect upon this important precept, in which their own honour as well as their children's happiness is so much at stake! The foolish mother may think she is securing to herself the love and affection of her favourite child when she is pleasing him with the sight of the bird fluttering in the cage; and may affectedly laugh at the impertinence and novel correction of any one that attempts to reprove her

---

[1] Prov. iii. 16.

folly or convince her of her mistake; for *like as a partridge taken and kept in a cage, so is the heart of the proud* (Ecclus. xi. 30). The proud heart of the mother is as unwilling to bear reproof, as the partridge to be confined in a cage. But, for my own part, I think that both the mother and the child are real objects of pity; for the parent knows not what she is doing, and that she is teaching her child the rudiments of undutifulness to herself, and dishonour to the family; and *as the cage is full of birds, so is her house full of deceit* (Jerem. v. 27).

St. Paul observes (Eph. vi. 2) that the commandment *honour thy father and mother* is the first commandment with *promise*. He thought the promise of prosperity and length of days was the best security to the observance of it. And surely the blessing can lose nothing of its excellence, because annexed to the precept *Let the dam go,* which after the apostle I may call the second commandment with promise. What God hath been pleased to join together with the very same promise, let not the folly or cruelty of man put asunder. Oh mother, think upon this golden chain of innumerable links of days of prosperity! For thy own, and thy child's sake, preserve it inviolable. If you truly love your child, instruct him in the mercy, and fear of God. The two commandments, *Honour thy parents* and *Let the dam go,* are more closely connected than you perhaps are willing to suppose. But revolve, I pray you, in your mind, the case of some family of your acquaintance, where the peace of it has been disturbed by the undutifulness and obstinacy of the children; and I believe you will find, that the parents have not a little contributed thereto, by not timely restraining their children from acts of sportive cruelty to birds and insects. Possibly they will not acknowledge that this was the cause of it. Few parents will confess themselves to have been in the wrong. The blame is generally laid upon the perverse disposition of the children, when yet that very perverseness is frequently chargeable to the parents' account. The minds of children are naturally tender, and susceptible of soft and benevolent impressions; and if some are of a rougher cast than others, they are still capable of being instructed in their duty, and reduced to order by the principles of religion, the fear of God, and trust in his promises. On the ground of religion, and of nature, parents may lay a sure foundation of reverential honour and filial love to themselves. But if you suffer your child to commit any acts of cruelty, you harden him against fear and every soft impression; you overthrow the foundation, and mar all the materials of thy family structure. For how can you think your child will fear and honour God, when you teach him to disregard the *promises* of God? Or how can you think that he will fear and honour *you*, when you teach him neither to fear nor honour God? You have discharged him from all obedience to thyself by permitting him to transgress a commandment, enjoined by the same authority, and recommended with the very same blessing, as the commandment of reverence to parents. You have taught him to trifle and quibble with the promise that links the two commandments together. How then can you expect that your child should obey you on the religious principle, that God has promised life and prosperity to such obedience, when you teach him to make light of this very promise in the other instance? And if your child regards you not from a religious principle, what is there left? Love and affection he can have none. For by your indulging him in wantonly catching of birds, tormenting of flies, spinning of beetles etc. you have rendered his once tender heart obdurate to the delicate feelings of pity and compassion.[1] And you can hardly suppose that he will have any concern about your pretended affection towards him, or your mournful complaints that he neither loves you, nor cares for you. No, it is *you*

---

[1] Similar sentiments are to be found in other eighteenth-century writers, sometimes inspired by John Locke's *Thoughts on Education* of 1693. Ten years after Primatt's work, Sarah Trimmer published her *The History of the Robins* which commenced the long tradition of anti-cruelty literature for children. R.D.R.

that have done this cruel work for thyself. You have nipped every bud of love. You have quenched every spark of affection. You have made him deaf to the voice of nature, by deafening his ears to the cries of the creatures. And at last you will find, as others have experienced before, that your foolish indulgence has taught him to be as insensible to your own pains and tears, as you have taught him to be insensible to the pains and misery of tormented birds and insects.

The child that can with indifference pull off the leg or wing of a fly, will in time, with the same indifference and hardheartedness, pull off the leg or wing of a bird, or the tail of a cat. He may indeed love his favourite dog more than he loves his mother; and no great wonder if he does. But he will throw stones at a neighbour's horse, or cut off the teats of a cow. It availeth not that the blessed Jesus made his solemn entry into Jerusalem *meek and lowly, and riding upon an ass*;[1] for as oft as the cruel wretch shall meet with his humble and inoffensive brute, he will be sure to give a testimony of his own infidelity by repeated mockeries and insults. Nor shall the bird of repentance be less the object of his malice than the beast of humility; and that too (as if in despite of the established religion) in the very season set apart by the Church for the purposes of humiliation and penance. St. Peter denied his master, the cock awakened him unto repentance; but repentance is an irksome task; therefore shall the cock be tied by the leg to a stake, and thrown at with cudgels till every bone in his body is broken; or, to make him a complete Cock of the Game, his stately crest must be cut off, and his spurs pared away for weapons of steel, and public notice given that the very objects and beasts of the people, who delight in blood, *may gather themselves together, and rejoice in his adversity*.[2] But if there be such a thing as relative holiness, or if there be any two animals more sacred than others, I would say they are

[1] Zech. ix. 9.   Matt. xxi. 5.
[2] Ps. xxxv. 15.

this bird of repentance, and the before mentioned beast of humility: or if there be any barbarous sport that is a particular scandal or disgrace to Christianity, I would say it is cockthrowing:[1] but *Woe be to them through whom the offence cometh.*[2] Yet it is by these unrestrained practices that the heart of youth is hardened; and from the wing of a fly to the teat of a cow, we may trace his procedure from one degree of cruelty to another, till at length humanity itself must bear the weight of his oppression and tyranny; and regardless of the cries of nature, or the ties of blood, he verifies the observation of the wise king of Israel, that as *he that is merciful doeth good to his own soul, so he that is cruel troubleth his own flesh,* (Prov. xi. 17).

Cruelty then, like other sins, has its progress and stages;[3] but being the devil's darling, it stands at the head of the black catalogue of sins. It is the very first sin that we read of in scripture after the fall of man; and though the overt acts may be suppressed, yet whilst it lurks in the heart, it lays the foundation of every act of mischief and injustice. A man that violates nature by any act of wanton cruelty, how trifling soever the object, can have no fear of God, no true principle of justice or honour. He can *neither do justly, nor love mercy, nor walk humbly with God.* Even in the smallest instances of it, he discovers a malevolence of heart dangerous to society. When Domitian was first advanced to the imperial throne of Rome, he amused himself in killing and tormenting of flies. We might else wonder how it was possible for a man to be guilty of the barbarities which he practised on his own subjects; but the wonder ceases when we are told that Domitian was cruel to a fly. The object was changed, but the subject was the same.

[1] This cruel sport was particularly a feature of the debaucheries associated with Shrove Tuesday. The Rev. Richard Humphries suggests a pre-Christian origin. R.D.R.
[2] Matt. xviii. 7.
[3] William Hogarth, strongly sympathetic to the animals' cause, had published his *The Four Stages of Cruelty* in 1750. R.D.R.

THE DUTY OF MERCY

It does not become any man to dictate to his superiors, but I cannot help sometimes supposing that if all the barbarous customs and practices still subsisting amongst us, were decreed to be as *illegal* as they are *sinful*, we should not hear of so many shocking murders and acts of inhumanity, as we now do. There have been governments (not the less wise I presume for this reason) that deemed cruelty to brutes a crime unworthy of men, and cognizable by law. It was one of the laws of Triptolemus: *Hurt no living creature*.[1] "History tells us of a wise and polite nation that rejected a person of the first quality, who stood for a judicatory office, only because he had been observed in his youth to take pleasure in tearing and murdering of birds; and of another that expelled a man out of the Senate, for dashing a bird against the ground, which had taken shelter in his bosom. Every one knows how remarkable the Turks are for their humanity in this kind."[2] And I have somewhere read that the pious Musselmen esteem it a duty of religion to purchase captive birds out of the cages of the Christians, that they may set them at liberty. These bowels of mercies in heathen and infidel nations ought surely to make Christians blush, when we compare their humanity and tenderness with our own. But we have so long accustomed ourselves to brutal cruelty, that our very nature seems transformed through vicious habit: the divine image, after which we were created, is effaced; our hearts are grown callous; and our judgment is as perverse as our heart.

But whatever may be the depravity or perverseness of the human heart, we read in the prophecy of Isaiah, that when the branch shall grow out of the root of Jesse, *the wolf shall dwell with the lamb, and the leopard shall lie down with the kid; and the calf and the young lion and the fatling together; and a little child shall lead them. And the cow and the bear shall feed; their young ones shall lie down together: and the lion shall eat straw*

---

[1] *Archæol. Græe.* B. i. Ch. 26.
[2] Guardian, No. 61.

like the ox. And the sucking child shall play on the hole of the asp, and the weaned child shall put his hand on the cockatrice (or adder's) *den. They shall not hurt nor destroy ...* (Isaiah xi. 6, 9). Some interpret this prophecy in the literal sense; and others have thought it is to be understood in a figurative sense, to denote that by the preaching of the gospel of Christ, the minds and tempers of men would be reformed, and the most untoward dispositions would become meek and gentle. But whether this prophecy is to be interpreted in a literal or in a figurative sense; whether it is to be applied to the natural or to the moral world; if it is a good method to judge of the time of the accomplishment of a prophecy by the coincidence of the event, we shall find it hard to determine how this has as yet been fulfilled. For savage brutes continue to be savage; and men are not much better. Either, then, we have mistaken the day of his coming; or (as the Jews tell us) he would have appeared at the appointed time, but the sins of men withheld him; or (and which as a Christian I conclude to be the case) he hath appeared, the root hath long since shot forth the branch, and the blessed event would long since have taken place, both literally and figuratively, in the natural world as well as in the moral world, if men would permit the branch to grow; that is, if Christians would be come Christians indeed, and by their good example engage *all the kingdoms of this world to become the kingdoms of our Lord and of his Christ* (Rev. xi. 15). But natural evil is so closely connected with moral evil, that until sin be taken away, the effect of sin must continue. If men would learn to fear God, and to observe his laws; if the Earth were *full of the knowledge of the Lord as the waters cover the sea*,[1] nature herself would wear another face. All would be peace, harmony and love. Men would become merciful; savage brutes would become tame; and the tame brutes would no more groan under the lash, and bear the weight of the sins of men; but all, both men and

---

[1] Isaish xi. 9.

brutes, would experience the blessing of the renovating change. When the lion *shall eat straw like the ox*, as he once did,[1] the lion will be tame as the ox; but so long as there is a disobedient prophet in Bethel,[2] so long must the lion retain his fierceness as a terror and executioner of God's judgement; and so long must his fierceness be supported and fed with the invigorating blood of the slain.

But these sheep, what have they done? Why should innocent cattle suffer because of the sins of men? I answer by a similar question: Why should innocent children suffer for the sins of wicked parents? When the house is overthrown, the whole family must perish. For though God may spare Nineveh for a while, for the sake of the innocent children and cattle, yet, if Nineveh will not repent, the innocent cattle must fall in the general ruin, but as *guiltless* as the innocent children *which cannot discern between their right hand and their left hand* (Jonah iv. 11).

Till we are able to account why innocent children should suffer for the sins of others, let it not be particularly alleged as the objection to the mercy of God towards the brutes, that the brutes should suffer likewise. His mercy ought no more to be called in question in the one case, than in the other; nor to a considerate mind will it be questioned in either case. For, indeed, it can hardly be avoided in public distress, but that the children must some way or other feel the effect of it; and for the same reason we are not to wonder that the brutes of humanity, who are connected with us, and dependent upon us, and who live as it were under our roof, are many times unhappily involved in the calamities which befall mankind. And if this be an evil, to the score of sinful men be it charged, and not to any wrath or displeasure in God towards the innocent and unsinning brutes, any more than to the innocent

---

[1] And God said ... *To every beast of the Earth ... I have given every green herb for meat.* Gen. i. 30.
[2] 1 Kings xiii. 24.

and unsinning babes; for *shall not the judge of all the Earth do right?* (Gen. xviii. 25).

Be this then the general answer to all objections of this kind. Yet see the perverseness and unreasonableness of sinful men. We first call down the vengeance of heaven, by our sins, to consume us in his wrath, and then we arraign the mercy of God, because those that are connected with us, perish in the flame which our own follies have kindled. But if it be true that the innocent must suffer with the guilty, it maketh sin to be more exceeding sinful; and this consideration ought to make us more careful how we offend, because when we fall, we fall not alone, for *in our skirts is found the blood of the souls of the poor innocents*;[1] and we aggravate our own sins by the miseries which we know the just punishment thereof must bring upon others.

And yet the mercy of God towards the innocent may sometimes be traced even in his judgments upon the wicked. For though the idea of death may be terrible to the living, yet, in itself, it hath no sting but for the sinner; nor hath the law any strength but for the transgressor. In the hands of God alone are the issues of life and of death, of blessing and of cursing; and he knows best how long he shall continue to any creature the blessing of life. But when *the day of the Lord is near, or the voice of the day of the Lord, a day of wrath, a day of trouble and distress, a day of wasteness and desolation;* when *he will bring distress upon men because they have sinned against the Lord;* and when *the whole land shall be devoured by the fire of his jealousy*,[2] it is in his mercy that by the medium of instant death, he taketh away the innocent from the evil to come; or if some innocents should be reserved, to procrastinate the day of vengeance for a time (as in the case of Nineveh), and at last to fall in the general wreck, to make the calamity the more exemplary and more affecting to others; yet, though they fall with the guilty, they fall not as the

[1] Jerem. ii. 24.
[2] Zeph. i. 14-17.

THE DUTY OF MERCY

victims of vengeance. To the unsinning beast, to the spotless babe, and to the righteous man, death is no further an evil than as it is the period of life; and when life would become a burthen, death becomes a blessing to all but to the sinner.

Suppose we now the day of distress at hand, and the blessing of death decreed. The unoffending brute must die; and what matters it to him, whether in the earthquake, or in a deluge, or in a slaughter-house? The helpless child must die; for should it survive the fall of its parents, it would be exposed to all the miseries of cold and famine; *the tongue of the sucking child cleaveth to the roof of his mouth for thirst: the young children ask bread, and no man breaketh it unto them.*[1] But God is pleased to take them away by the sudden point of the sword, not more painful than the tedious cutting of the teeth. The righteous man too must die, and *he seemeth to die* in pain: *In the sight of the unwise, his departure is taken for misery; and his going away to be utter destruction; yet he is in peace: and though he may seem to be punished in the sight of men, yet is his hope full of immortality; and having been a little chastised, he shall be greatly rewarded* (Wisdom iii. 2, 3, 4).

According to the foregoing supposition, in the day of public calamity the same event of untimely death befalls the righteous man, the helpless babe, and the unoffending brute. Now if the man and the babe are not exempted, I presume there is no occasion for me to endeavour to prove that the more favour ought to be shown to the innocent brute than to the innocent man. If it is in his *mercy* that God taketh away the man; it can be no impeachment of his mercy that the brute dieth likewise. But suppose it were in *wrath*; whatever evil may ensue, to the account of wicked men be placed all the dismal charge. For as the God of nature is the God of grace, and as the same God who was the creator of the world is the moral governor of it, I am emboldened to say, on the principles of divine revelation, that nature

[1] Lam. iv. 4.

would never have groaned if man had not sinned. If the brutes then suffer through our sins, upon ourselves be their misery; we are the occasion of it all; for *when the land mourneth, and the herbs of every field wither, for the wickedness of them that dwell therein, the beasts and the birds are consumed* (Jerem. xii. 4).

See here the dire effect of sin. The land mourneth, the herbs wither, the brutes perish; and why? *For the wickedness of them that dwell in the land.* Say not then that God is unmerciful to the brutes; but say, rather, that the unmercifulness and cruelty is in man, who provoketh the Almighty to curse the land, which would otherwise produce food sufficient for all the inhabitants thereof; and what little is reserved for the beast or the bird, is devoured by the men through whom the calamity cometh.

In this manner might we in some measure account for the miseries which befall the innocent. It is their misfortune to be connected with the guilty; but the general mercy of God towards all his creatures is no more to be called in question for this, than the justice of a wise legislature is to be arraigned because, in the punishment of a criminal, the effect of his crime may extend to his innocent family. The law doth not punish the innocent; but if the innocent suffer for the guilty, charge that suffering to the account of the criminal. And yet, after all that has been said, I firmly believe that no evil which the innocent brutes suffer from the hand of God on the account of men, is in any respect equal to the pains and miseries they endure from the cruelties of men. For God is merciful even when provoked to judgment, but man is cruel without any provocation at all. Let me fall, saith David, *into the hand of the Lord; for his mercies are great: and let me not fall into the hand of man* (2 Sam. xxiv. 14).

When the wickedness of men was so great in the Earth that God was determined to destroy the whole race of mankind (the inclosed in the ark only excepted), his mercy was conspicuous even in his judgment. For the sake of the few men that were to be saved, it seemed expedient that the brutes should perish; for had they all been spared, the disproportion of numbers between men and brutes in the new world would probably have occasioned various inconveniences. The multitude of the savage beasts would have been a continual terror to the new race of men, and the multitude of the tamer kind would have been as straggling sheep without a shepherd. Born to die once, their term of life indeed was shortened; but the manner of their death by water was, upon the whole, more easy to many of them, and more expeditious than if the tame brutes had been devoured by the fierce, and the fierce had perished by lingering famine. Had it been by general fire, it would have consumed the fishes of the sea, as well as the creatures of the Earth; and it would have made a greater havoc in the creation than was necessary to accomplish the end proposed; nor would the ark itself have been spared. But as God was not angry with the brutes, water was the merciful expedient to save no less than to destroy. The waters prevailed, *and every living substance was destroyed which was upon the face of the ground, both man, and cattle, and the creeping things, and the fowl of the heaven; and they were destroyed from the Earth* (Gen. vii. 23).

But God *remembered Noah, and every living creature, and all the cattle that was with him in the ark* (Gen. viii. 1). God remembered the brutes that were shut up, as well as the men; and *made a wind to pass over the Earth, and the waters assuaged.* And *the Lord sent forth his spirit, and renewed the face of the Earth*[1]. He looked upon the desolation, and it seemed to have repented him that the brutes had perished; and that which had been the motive of judgment he now declares shall never move him again to blot the innocent brutes out of his creation for the sins of guilty men. Read, and adore his love, and see how his mercy rejoiceth against judgment: *The Lord said in his heart, I will not again curse the ground any more for man's sake; for the*

[1] Ps. civ. 30.

imagination of man's heart is evil from his youth; neither will I again smite any more every living thing, as I have done (Gen. viii. 21).

Nor was it enough that the Lord *said it in his heart,* but graciously condescends to bind himself by a covenant; by an everlasting covenant, not confined to any family, to any nation, to any church; no, nor to *human* kind; but a covenant as extensive as it is eternal, as merciful as it is magnificent, and as sublime in the form of it, as it is astonishingly beautiful in the seal and signature. And to convince Noah of all future generations, that *the mercy of the Lord is over all his works*; and that every living creature, of the fowl, of the cattle and of every beast of the Earth, is as much, in its kind, the object of his loving kindness as man, yea more than *sinful* man; and that it was not in his wrath to the unsinning brutes which had perished, that he had swept them away in the general flood; he is moreover most graciously pleased to take in the surviving brutes for themselves, and for their posterities, as parties jointly interested with men, and expressly named together with them in the same everlasting covenant, written in heaven, and sealed with the rainbow.

Behold the form of the covenant, and bear witness unto the token visible to all men even unto this day:

THE COVENANT

*God spake unto Noah,
and to his Sons with him, saying:
And I, behold I establish
my covenant
with you, and
with your seed after you,
and with every
living creature
that is with you, of the
fowl, of the cattle,
and of every beast of the Earth
with you,*

from all that go out of the ark,
to every beast of the Earth.
And
I will establish my covenant with you;
neither shall all flesh be cut off
any more by the waters of a flood:
Neither shall there any more be a flood
to destroy the Earth.

Gen. ix. 8-11.

THE TOKEN

And God said:
This is the Token of the Covenant
which I make between Me and You,
and every Living Creature that is with you,
for perpetual generations:
I do set my bow in the cloud,
and it shall be for a token of a Covenant
between Me and the Earth.
And it shall come to pass,
when I bring a cloud over the Earth, that
the bow shall be seen in the cloud:
And I will remember my Covenant
which is between Me, and You,
and every Living Creature of all flesh;
and the waters shall no more become a flood
to destroy all flesh.
And the bow shall be in the cloud;
and I will look upon it, that I may remember
The Everlasting Covenant
between God and every living creature
of all flesh, that is upon the Earth.
And God said unto Noah,
this is the
Token of the Covenant,
which I have established between me
and all flesh that is upon the Earth.

Gen. ix. 12-17.

Look upon the rainbow, and praise him that made it;[1] and let that beautiful and resplendent arch of heaven be the visible memorial of the Lord throughout the generations, that his mercy is over all his works.

I presume it is now unnecessary that I should add any more arguments or testimonies to those which have been already advanced and produced. For what? Shall God establish his covenant, his everlasting covenant with every living creature, of the fowl, of the cattle, and of every beast of the Earth, as well as with man? And shall we despise those creatures, which are no less than ourselves in covenant with God? Shall God spare a wicked city for the sake of beast as well as babe? And shall we abuse those creatures for whose sake (perhaps) our city and our land is spared? Shall God display the riches of his goodness in his creation of, and in his providential care over, the beasts of the Earth, and over the fowls of the air, and over the fishes of the sea, and over every living creature that moveth upon the Earth, which his wisdom and goodness hath created and made? Shall he confirm the common dictates of humanity and natural religion, by the express declarations of his holy word, by promises, by threatenings, by precepts, and by examples, recorded in scripture for our learning? And shall any man dare to say or presume to suppose that God regardeth them not? No, saith the Wisdom of Solomon: *Thou lovest all the things that are, and abhorrest nothing that thou hast made; for never wouldst thou have made any thing if thou hadst hated it; and how could any thing have endured, if it had not been thy will? Or been preserved, if not called by thee* (Wisd. xi. 24). *Thy power is the beginning of righteousness; and because thou art the Lord of all, it maketh thee to be gracious unto all* (Ch. xii. 16).

As I have just now quoted an apocryphal writing, I will take up my song of praise with Ananias, Azarias and Misael:

O Ye whales, and all that move in the waters, bless ye

---

[1] Ecclus. xliii. 11.

THE DUTY OF MERCY

the Lord; praise and exalt him above all for ever.

O all ye fowls of the air, bless ye the Lord; praise and exalt him above all for ever.

O all ye beasts and cattle, bless ye the Lord; praise and exalt him above all for ever.

O ye children of men, bless ye the Lord; praise and exalt him above all for ever.

O ye holy and humble men of heart, bless ye the Lord; praise and exalt him above all for ever.

O give thanks unto the Lord, because he is gracious; for his mercy endureth for ever.

CHAPTER FIVE

AND now, upon a candid review of the numerous passages of holy scripture, which I have collected into this treatise, and on some of which I have enlarged (not with any design to fatigue or mislead my reader, but only to imprint them the more deeply in his mind), give me leave to ask if it is possible that any man, who acknowledges the authority of the sacred writings, and duly considers the gracious and merciful intent and force of these passages, can be insensible either of the goodness of God, or of the duty of mercy, or the sin of cruelty, towards the brute animals? To me, I freely own, they appear so strong and irresistible that I cannot but think that he who professes to be a Christian, and yet is negligent as to this important duty of mercy, must be either very ignorant of the genuine principles of the gospel, which is the utmost perfection of the law, or must have a heart hardened to an uncommon degree.

We may pretend to what religion we please, but cruelty is atheism. We may make our boast of Christianity; but cruelty is infidelity. We may trust to our orthodoxy; but cruelty is the worst of heresies. The religion of Christ Jesus originated in the mercy of God; and it was the gracious design of it to promote peace to every creature upon Earth, and to create a spirit of universal benevolence or *goodwill* in men.[1] And as it pleased God therein to display the riches of his own goodness and mercy towards us; and the revealer of his blessed will, the author and finisher of our faith, hath commanded us to be *merciful, as our father also is merciful*, the obligation upon Christians becomes the

[1] Luke ii. 14.

THE DUTY OF MERCY

stronger; and it is our bounden duty, in an especial manner, and above all other people, to extend the precept of mercy to every object of it. For, indeed, a cruel Christian is a monster of ingratitude, a scandal to his profession, and beareth the name of Christ in vain: and in vain will he plead the mercies of God in Christ Jesus, when he appeareth before the God of universal nature. *As is the majesty of the Lord so is his mercy*[1] *unto merciful men, whose righteousness shall not be forgotten.*[2] But, *as his mercy is great, so is his correction also; for he judgeth a man according to his works.*[3] Cruelty will debar mercy even in the father of mercies, and cut off all hope even in the *God of all comfort.* He that *hath showed no mercy, shall have judgment without mercy;*[4] and, in the righteous judgment of God, he will at length be forced to confess with Adonibezek: *As I have done, so God hath requited me* (Judges i. 7).

Let me intreat thee, then, O courteous Christian reader, by all that is amiable, just, and good; let me intreat thee for God's sake, for Christ's sake, for man's sake, for beast's sake, yea, and for thine own sake, *put on (as an elect of God, holy and beloved) bowels of mercies, kindness, humbleness of mind, meekness.*[5] Make it your business, esteem it your duty, believe it to be the ground of your hope, and know that it is that which the Lord doth require of thee – *to do justly, and to love mercy, and to walk humbly with thy God.* See that no brute of any kind, whether intrusted to thy care, or coming in thy way, suffer through thy neglect or abuse. Let no views of profit, no compliance with custom, and no fear of the ridicule of the world, ever tempt thee to the least act of cruelty or injustice to any creature whatsoever. But let this be your invariable

[1] Ecclus. ii. 18.
[2] Ecclus. xliv. 10.
[3] xvi. 12.
[4] James ii. 13.
[5] Col. iii. 12.

AND SIN OF CRUELTY TO BRUTE ANIMALS

rule, everywhere, and at all times, to *do unto others as, in their condition, you would be done unto.*

After this general precept, all further rules for thy conduct are unnecessary. I shall therefore add no more than to exhort thee to *be merciful as God is merciful; to be merciful as you hope for mercy; and to receive with reverence and attention the blessing of the Lord Jesus Christ.*

Blessed are the merciful for they shall obtain mercy.